EASY

TASTY

ITALIAN

ADD SOME MAGIC

TO YOUR

EVERYDAY FOOD

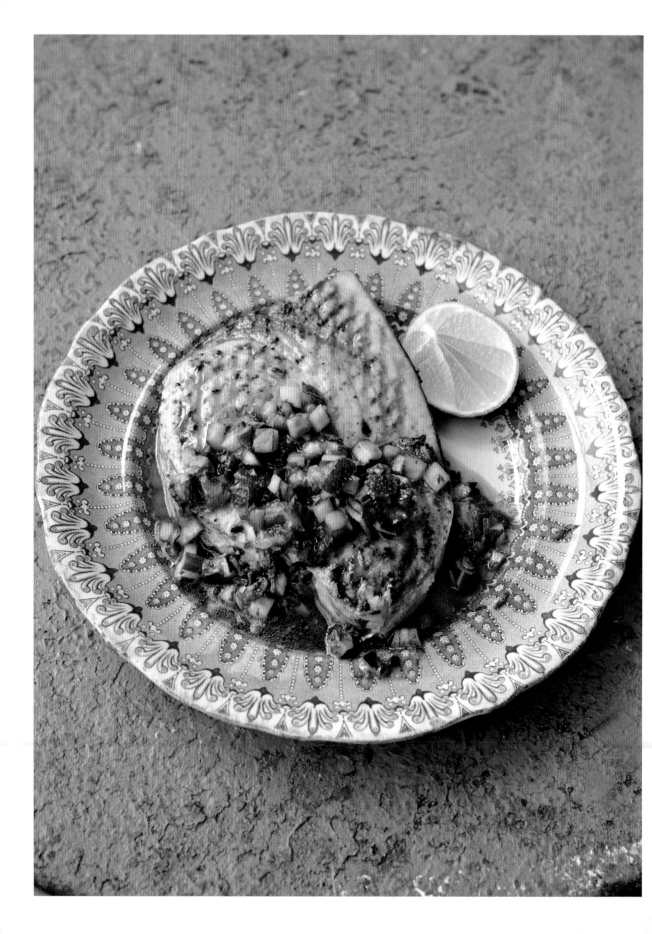

EASY

TASTY

ITALIAN

ADD SOME MAGIC

TO YOUR

EVERYDAY FOOD

Laura

Santtini

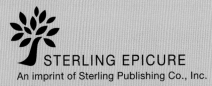

STERLING EPICURE

An imprint of Sterling Publishing Co., Inc.

New York / London

www.sterlingpublishing.com

PHOTOGRAPHS BY
SIMON WHEELER

For Christopher, the alchemist whose golden
heart and light transformed my life, and for
Mathilda and Giacomo, who are my life.

STERLING and the distinctive Sterling logo are registered trademarks of
Sterling Publishing Co., Inc.

10 9 8 7 6 5 4 3 2 1

Published in 2010 by
Sterling Publishing Co., Inc.
387 Park Avenue South,
New York, NY 10016

First published in 2009 by
Quadrille Publishing Limited,
Alhambra House, 27–31 Charing Cross Road,
London WC2H OLS

EDITORIAL DIRECTOR Jane O'Shea
CREATIVE DIRECTOR Helen Lewis
EDITOR AND PROJECT MANAGER Lewis Esson
DESIGNER Jim Smith
PHOTOGRAPHY Simon Wheeler
STYLING & FOOD FOR PHOTOGRAPHY Laura Santtini
PRODUCTION Vincent Smith, Marina Asenjo

Sterling ISBN: 978-1-4027-8055-4

Printed and bound in China.

IMPORTANT NOTES
All recipes serve 4 unless otherwise stated.
The author suggests using edible metals in certain recipes. This is a suggestion
and not a recommendation, and the use and consumption of such metals is
at your own risk. Neither the author nor the publisher accept any liability for
any illness, harm, or injury arising from the use or consumption of such metals.
Always read labels, warnings, and directions on the packaging of such products
before use.

CONTENTS

FOREWORD

by Gillian Riley, food historian and author of *The Oxford Companion to Italian Food*

Cooking and eating with Laura is always an adventure–shock and awe and pleasant surprises lurk within the kitchen and upon the plate. She has her head in rose-scented clouds, glittering with magical effusions, and her feet firmly on the ground, steady as a rock, anchored by a lifetime's professionalism and skills learned the hard way. The sparks fly, but the fire extinguisher of common sense keeps them under control. Dreams and portents come in and out of focus until a tried-and-tested recipe emerges. Imagination and inspiration are tamed by down-to-earth cooking, just as the arcane contents of the alchemist's flask vaporize and then condense into a clear and (hopefully) wholesome liquid.

This book looks at the traditions and ingredients of Italian cooking and shows how we can enjoy both continuity and innovation. It uses the ideas of the alchemists and the techniques of generations of grannies and whiz-kids. It is not a 'how to' book, a step-by-step, auto-repair-manual approach to Italian gastronomy–there are plenty of those around–but an approach to cooking that demands intelligence and creativity in its application, rather than blind obedience. And all the recipes work, whether they are the basic templates for a series of variations, or a one-off like the beef braised in Barolo or the Santini version of *osso buco*.

Throughout the history of Italian food, change and innovation have merged with time-honored practices, plenty of 'You should never, you must always …' from the old and wise, tempered by a sprinkling of subversive novelties from the iconoclastic young. Laura's manic use of spices and herbs is part of this heritage; the courtly cuisine of the Middle Ages used spices in abundance, lingering in the *Peperata* of her native Venice, and modified during the Renaissance, until a discrete powdering of sugar and cinnamon over a finished dish in 17th-century Naples was the last dying sigh of a robust tradition. When I was trying out Renaissance recipes decades ago, a neat way of getting this final touch was to whiz some sugar, salt, and cinnamon in a coffee grinder and waft it over fried chicken sprinkled with rose water. A distinguished printing historian dipped a finger in the mixture and pronounced: 'Renaissance stardust', and so, when I passed this notion by Laura, a star was born …

Spices went underground when the dead hand of French gastronomy spread like a phylloxera blight over European kitchens, imposing the dogma of a cuisine with different principles and seasonings upon the wide variety of regional Italian styles. But some free spirits like Vincenzo Corrado in Naples used local Italian ingredients in an inventive and subversive way, and spiced them up with more gusto than convention required. The mild-mannered doctor Giacomo Rajberti, working in Milan in the 1840s, used the Milanese dialect and some hearty traditional recipes to cock a snook at the hated occupying French. A generation later, Pellegrino Artusi, writing in pure Tuscan, produced the food bible of the rising bourgeoisie, a dumbing down of the robust cuisines of his native Emilia-Romagna and his adoptive city of Florence. It is claimed that he did more than Garibaldi or *I promessi sposi* for the reunification of Italy, as every literate middle-class lady in the peninsula found herself reading his lucid and avuncular prose. Artusi directed a sizeable chunk of the nation onto the same wavelength. But what Artusi did for the nation's cooking is less laudable: a smug middle-class blandness settled upon the palates of his grateful readers, and even now, well into the revival of regional food and the *cucina della nonna*, there is a reluctance to admit to the use of strong seasonings, and in some households an almost religious fear of garlic. Laura's approach blows all this out of the water with a revivalist fervor, and the robust flavors that have always perfumed the kitchens of Italy can now permeate the homes and gardens of all her readers, here and overseas.

The alchemists were down to earth in their techniques, but their arcane concept of the 'transformation' of base ingredients into new and wonderful substances is what all good cooks aim at, as we can read in the Introduction. The practicalities of cooking were also used by Mevlana, creator of the Sufi branch of Islam in the 13th century, to describe the mystic raptures of divine love in terms of everyday things, 'I was raw, I was cooked, I was burnt', he said of the soul's transformation, and admonished, 'Say nothing, froth not, do not raise the lid of the cauldron; simmer well, and be patient, for I am cooking you.' An appeal to a common experience in oriental cooking, where the lid keeps in the rich fragrances until the moment of perfect synthesis.

One of Mevlana's poems compares our errant souls to someone wandering in a bazaar:

> *Stay close, my heart, to the one who knows your ways,*
> *Come into the shade of the tree that always has fresh flowers.*
> *Don't stroll idly through the bazaar of the perfume-makers,*
> *Stay in the shop of the sugar-seller.*
> *If you don't find true balance, anyone can deceive you …*

True balance is what is aimed at in the recipes in this book, both the basic procedures and the variations on them. The unconventional structure is a deliberate departure from menu-based Italian cookery books, which follow either the sequence of dishes in a meal, from appetizers to desserts, or a conventional grouping of ingredients–fish, chicken, whatever. Here we have a different perspective, based on the pursuit of the amazing bursts of flavor that Italian cooks have been getting together since the beginning of time, and only recently analysed and diagnosed as *umami*, a Japanese name for a universal phenomenon. Different ways of presenting what the alchemists and the cooks of old were doing have inspired this new way of presenting the techniques and glories of Italian cooking, and so the sections of this book follow the logic of their activities, with the different ways of exploiting the umami, (*o mamma mia!*) of key ingredients and processes. Now we can use Laura's analysis and deconstruct the manifestations of umami, following the instinctive ways of her ancestors, who were getting bursts of flavor without bothering about the chemical structures of what they were doing. For example, the crunchy bits in a mouthful of Parmesan cheese are not salt crystals but pure umami, which explains why Parmesan gets to be added as a last-minute flavor-enhancer on meat, fish, and pasta, its use in stuffings, its surprising success in a sweet ice cream, and its

traditional role at the end of a meal in Emilia-Romagna, served in chunks anointed with a *battesimo* of *aceto balsamico tradizionale di Modena*. The ancient Romans used *garum* and *liquamen*, sauces and relishes made from rotted and fermented fish, similar to the *nam pla* of Thai cuisine today, to give saltiness and flavor to their cooking. This sauce did not survive the fall of Rome, but the use of salted anchovies persists in Italian cooking today, either dissolved in a *bagna cauda*, or as whole fillets athwart a pizza Napoletana, combining with cheese and tomato to give the umami effect.

A homely recipe for sea bass, where fillets are dusted with Parmesan, strewn with some fresh sage leaves, and wrapped in Parma ham, then sprinkled with grappa and baked in a hot oven for a short time, is umami in action. *Funghi porcini*, backed up with garlic and parsley, in a sauce for fresh egg tagliatelle, give resonance. So rather than reach for the little bottle of MSG, start using the ingredients that combine to give the taste-enhancing effects described by Laura: anchovies and fresh raw tomatoes, and garlic as a spaghetti sauce, or the deep, dark, sombre devil's brew of chocolate, chili, sesame, and sugar as elements in a wicked barbecue marinade. Flavors and textures—ways of preparing pastes, powders, rubs, and marinades, ways of cooking, and imaginative serving suggestions—are all presented here with wit and common sense. The alchemical notion of transformation is applied to the way ingredients become more than the sum of the parts of a recipe. The sage leaf and slice of Parma ham in *saltimbocca alla romana* give soul to bland veal *scallopine*, creating a new entity. The heart of *melanzane alla parmigiana* is not the melting mozzarella, but the generous layers of grated Parmesan that bring out the soft pungency of the eggplant. (Try Laura's version with 100% cacao powder for added oomph.)

Once readers have grasped the essentials, there is no fear of losing the plot. With understanding and a few basic skills, the thrill of achievement will be ours.

HUG ME, I'M HALF ITALIAN

I've kept a badge saying 'HUG ME I'M HALF ITALIAN' for over twenty years, I used to wear it just in case. Actually, I'm half Italian, a quarter Persian, a pinch of Sephardic and the rest is English-Irish, the genetic equivalent of a Molotov cocktail. Over four beliefs and cultures under one skin, an emotional suicide bomber, neither fish nor fowl.

Age has confirmed that every man wants a woman who is a chef in the kitchen, a lady in the parlor, and a whore in the bedroom. Trouble is, today most of us tend to be Gordon Ramsay throughout the house.

Forget Domestic Goddess. With five boys, three hotels, and a wayward husband, 'Nonna' Armelin Pasqua, my paternal grandmother and the best cook I knew, was a Domestic Sergeant Major–she had to be. My grandfather believed that if there was no visible action on the stove by 6 a.m., when he left the house, lunch was not worth coming home for. Wise to this excuse for a liquid lunch, Nonna Pasqua rose early to fill a selection of pots and pans with water and the odd rib of celery, all of which would be bubbling with false promise by daybreak.

It was in Nonna Pasqua's kitchen that I learnt my broken Venetian dialect, and how to skin, gut, and chop all things dead. She taught me to fish gnocchi out of the pan as soon as they bob to the surface, to skim the dirty foam from the top of the *bollito misto*, to grate nutmeg in the accompanying mashed potatoes; and that size does matter when it comes to a fist full of pudding rice. It was at her starch-stiffened table that I first scooped warm marrow from a bony Stonehenge and chased sauces round my plate with petals from my hollow bread rose. I helped where I could, the concept of a culinary wonderland crystallizing in my mind. I began to understand the power of food and temptation. It was Nonna who taught me, way before Joan Armatrading, to mix some water with my wine.

The biggest lesson was 'Waste not, want not'. Her reluctance to put anything in the bin led to the preparation of *cicciole* my absolute favorite treat. *Cicciole* (see pages 136–7) are made from any excess fatty skin on a chicken, usually from the neck or around the cavity opening. Nonna would slice these quilted remnants into small waxy strips and fry them in hot olive oil. I would watch, with my mouth watering, as they struggled and spat from the pan, then wait patiently as they rested on the yellow sugar paper, before munching them one by one with a sprinkling of salt. I fancy that if pigs could fly, their scratchings would taste more like this: crispy bits of heaven.

We moved to London in 1971 and my father opened a restaurant. The unfamiliar surroundings of our new home drove him to busman's weekends there, which he spent cooking. When I was not reading *Jackie* or dancing in front of the mirror to Showaddywaddy, I was his assistant. I remember gingerly pouring a steady stream of extra virgin olive oil on to a single yolk. We did not use mustard to mediate this unlikely match; snot-green mayonnaise was seasoned at the end, by me. Making mayonnaise is about a moment. It's about not giving away too much too soon. It's about recognizing that moment when things go wrong but are still redeemable. It's about knowing that you pushed things that little bit too far and dealing with the mess. It's about cutting your losses and making a thoroughly clean start. Eggs: if you can't beat 'em, chuck 'em.

I didn't know what bad food was until I started school in England, where in my first home economics lesson we were taught to wrap a grey hard-cooked egg in fluorescent-pink sausage meat and roll this in Paxo stuffing mix. I understood immediately why the lady next door had bought my dad that 'Italians Do It Better' T-shirt. Thirty years on things have changed, and today eclectic Britain does it better than anyone else in the world. The Enoch Powell school of cookery never took off, and there is no flavor, other than perhaps the family dog, that is not enjoyed at modern British tables. This has not always been the case, as I imagine that war, and the country's unrelenting recovery, had a lot to do with British cooking acquiring a bland reputation. My friend Harriett fondly remembers childhood meals in monochrome. The white meal, for example, would be plaice, cauliflower, boiled potatoes, and semolina. A disappointing crock at the end of a gourmet rainbow when there are records of Parmesan cheese and polenta being used in well-to-do kitchens as early as 1898.

Ingredients are important and, as a mother and cook, I believe in buying the best ingredients a household can afford. I am therefore inquisitive when it comes to provenance and loyal to the seasons. That said, it is possible to make a tasty dish for palate and purse literally out of a pig's ear. I often see women at the market collecting discarded vegetables. Those ladies have the power to transform one man's rubbish into another man's feast. Kitchens are about invention and the bubble and squeak of reinvention. That is the alchemy of cooking.

Laura Santtini
London, July 2009

EASY TASTY KNOW-HOW

Section 1

It's
not
pretty
being
easy

THE TOOLS OF TRANSFORMATION

In these few introductory pages I have set out lists of the equipment and ingredients that are at the heart of this book. These are definitely not in any way intended as shopping lists or 'must haves', rather they are the framework of the tapestry of wonderful food to explore later in the book. If we but had the technology, I would have wanted you to be able to lick these pages and get the flavor of all these magical ingredients to inspire you.

KITCHEN EQUIPMENT

Just before writing this page I went to check my kitchen to see what essential bits of equipment were required for kitchen wizardry at this level and this is what I found:

- a selection of kitchen knives gathered over the years, of all different shapes, sizes, makes, and degrees of bluntness;
- an old confit jar full of burnt, gnarled wooden spoons that were purchased when John Major was in Downing Street;
- a set of stainless-steel pots and pans with matching lids–a wedding gift that outlasted the marriage;
- a much-used nonstick frying pan in which I found a couple of slightly stained pastel-colored spatulas;
- two well-worn cast-iron casserole pots;
- a set of oven-to-tableware;
- and a couple of roasting pans and racks, that completed this motley collection.

A more extensive search revealed the rest of the usual suspects, some of which I had been looking for for years:

- an ancient pestle and mortar;
- a peeler, a cheese grater, chopping boards, a potato masher, salad spinner, lemon squeezer, metal sieve (with slightly melted handle), measuring jug, and so on.

The image was more yard sale than Domestic Goddess.

Tools of exceptional importance or beauty were few and far between. Only my designer pasta pot and food mixer are nominated in that category. The food processor, hand blender, and coffee grinder are all purely functional. Be safe in the knowledge that everything in this book can be, and has been, cooked with the sorry collection of tinker's trinkets listed above. Easy tasty cooking requires very little equipment other than your eyes, your hands, and a couple of ifs and ands.

However, here is a suggested capsule collection of kitchen must-haves to get you started:

- large pasta cooking pot with built-in colander and lid
- 2 nonstick frying pans, large and small
- set of stainless steel saucepans with lids
- round cast iron casserole, 8-inch (round is best for cooking risotto)
- roasting tray, 5½-inch
- large spoon
- assorted wooden spoons and spatulas
- kitchen scissors
- set of kitchen knives
- carving knife and fork
- large pestle and mortar (ideally granite with a rough interior)
- can opener
- large ladle
- potato masher
- set of tongs
- rolling pin
- balloon whisk
- chopping boards
- citrus squeezer
- mixing bowls, small and large
- large oven to table dish

'If ifs and ands were pots and pans, there'd be no work for tinkers' hands'

TYPICAL ITALIAN LARDER

I say 'typical' Italian larder because most larders these days are continuously transforming as ingredients travel freely all over the world. Epicurean immigrants, such as curry powder and pesto, comfortably inhabit cupboards stuffed with local ingredients far from their countries of origin.

With this in mind, I have drawn up a traditional Italian larder using the more typical produce. Don't be surprised, though, when visiting Italy if you find that modern cooks there are following Renaissance ancestors and including more exotic flavors and cooking methods.

However, I do believe that, even when experimenting, the root of the dish must be firmly located in the traditional blueprint of its original form before branching out into new realms of flavor.

BEANS AND LEGUMES (DRIED AND CANNED)
borlotti beans
cannellini beans
chick-peas
fava beans
lentils

CARBS
capellini
pastina
penne
rigatoni
spaghetti
polenta (instant)
risotto rice (Arborio)

CHEESES (IN THE REFRIGERATOR)
fontina
Gorgonzola
mascarpone
mozzarella

Parmesan
pecorino
ricotta

CURED MEATS
bresaola
cotechino
mortadella
pancetta
prosciutto crudo and cotto
salame
salsiccia (sausage)

DRIED BREAD CRUMBS AND NUTS
dried apricots
almonds
hazelnuts
pine nuts
pistachio nuts
raisins
walnuts

DRIED HERBS AND SEASONINGS
bay leaves
cloves
fennel seeds
juniper berries
myrtle
oregano
rosemary
sage
thyme
dried red chili flakes
peperoncino (chili)
dried porcini (cèpe) mushrooms
black peppercorns
pink peppercorns
saffron strands
rock salt, salt flakes and table salt

FRESH HERBS (IN POTS)
basil
bay leaves
fennel
marjoram
mint

(flat-leaf) parsley
rosemary
sage
tarragon
thyme

OTHER JARS AND CANS
anchovies in olive oil (not the white/grey sort that have not been salted)
clams in brine
white tuna in olive oil
artichoke hearts, bottled
black olives (Taggiascha)
green olives
black-olive paste
green-olive paste
capers (either salted or pickled in vinegar)
caper berries
chili paste (not easy to find but, if you do, grab it; otherwise I use harissa)
roasted bell peppers, bottled
pesto
tomato paste
passata (tomato pulp)
canned Italian plum tomatoes (best-value item ever!)
sun-dried tomatoes

OILS AND VINEGARS
olive oil: quality extra virgin for using raw
olive oil: ordinary olive oil for cooking
balsamic vinegar DOP
red wine vinegar
white wine vinegar

WINES AND SPIRITS
Campari
grappa
Marsala
red and white wines
vermouth

THE UMAMI LARDER

Umami fills the intensely savory things that make you go 'mmmmm'. It is in that bit of chicken skin stuck to the bottom of the roasting tray, that salty anchovy that melts into the tomato on a pizza, or the irresistible creamy combination of pancetta and Parmesan in a carbonara.

Discovered in 1908 by the Japanese, umami is the fifth taste –it was only eventually accepted recently by Western scientists, when they could find it had its own receptors on the tongue. Previously only sweet, sour, salty, and bitter had been universally recognized, as their individual receptors had been identified, but the umami receptors were cleverly hidden away inside the receptors for sweetness.

Even though this fifth taste remained unrecognized for so long, it has been instinctively exploited throughout time to enhance and intensify the pleasure of food in every country and culture. From the fermented fish condiment *liquamen/garum* used by ancient civilizations, to the cheeseburger-and-ketchup combination of today, the fifth taste has literally been an invisible delight on the tip of mankind's tongue since he had one.

Umami is a Japanese name for 'deliciousness', but refers only to the intensely savory taste imparted by glutamates (salts of the amino acid glutamic acid, found naturally bound with protein in foods) and five ribonucleotides, including inosinate and guanylate, which occur naturally in many foods, including meat, fish, vegetables, and dairy products.

Interestingly, if you match two very different ingredients recognized to be high in umami, such as (glutamate-containing) tomatoes with (inosinate-containing) minced beef, the combined umami can be increased up to the power of eight. Apply this 1 + 1 = 8 formula to a simple spaghetti bolognese topped with Parmesan cheese and you have one of the most potent flavor bombs in the world.

That is why the carrot, onion, and celery *soffritto* base explored on page 84 plays such a key role in Italian cookery. When these glutamate-packed ingredients are combined with foods that are naturally high in inosinates, such as meat and fish, the magic is done, and a dish with eight times more flavor than the sum of its parts is created. Those invisible and transformational six extra flavor points represent much of the hidden magic within this book.

To top it all, Parmigiano Reggiano is the Italian national cheese and ranks among the most powerful conveyors of umami in the world. Although the Italians left the 'official' discovery of umami to the Japanese, this king of cheeses has provided last-minute 'extra' umami for hundreds of years, assuring that the words *Buon Appetito* were never left to chance!

I have christened umami found in the Italian kitchen U-mamma! The main carriers of Italian 'deliciousness' are listed in this larder on the right.

U-MAMMA!

IN THE ITALIAN LARDER

salted anchovies
tomatoes
prosciutto crudo
Parmesan cheese
porcini (cep) mushrooms
white truffles
balsamic vinegar
meat extracts

CONDIMENTS

Knorr Aromat Seasoning
Maggi Seasoning Sauce
Bovril yeast extract
Marmite yeast extract
Kraft Vegemite yeast extract
fish sauce
Geo Watkins Anchovy Sauce
Geo Watkins Mushroom Ketchup
Lea & Perrins Worcestershire Sauce
Patum Peperium–Gentleman's Relish
miso
Oxo stock cube
parloa bean
sauerkraut
soy sauce
concentrated tomato
tomato extract
tomato ketchup

OTHERS

green tea

I LOVE THE TASTE OF YOU

ONE, TWO, THREE, FOUR, FIVE,
ONCE I LOVED A MAN WHO LIED,
SIX, SEVEN, EIGHT, NINE, TEN,
THEN I LET HIM GO AGAIN.

THE ALCHEMIC LARDER

Venice is the capital of the Veneto, the region from which my family came. One can only imagine the splendor of *La Serenissima* in her heyday. Ships would set sail to trade with the Middle East and Byzantium, returning laden with the heady, the precious, and the magical. Venice fast became the center for all things delicious, from salt to silk and grains to gold. Similarly, the East meets the West in my soul. I am a living cocktail of cultures and tastes, of hope-filled journeys, foreign adventure, and unexpected love. These ingredients are the magic and the madness in my life that sent me on an exploration of alchemy and the possibility of transformation.

PRECIOUS METALS
edible gold (see page 40)
edible silver (see page 40)

DRIED FLORALS
hibiscus flowers
jasmine flowers
lavender flowers
orange flowers
rose petals
violet flowers

FRUITS
Amalfi lemon
barberries
bitter orange
pomegranate
sour black cherries
wild strawberries

NUTS & SEEDS
bitter walnuts
pistachios
scorched almonds
sweet hazelnuts
poppy seeds
sesame seeds

ELIXIRS
honey
mosto cotto (cooked grape must)
orange water
pomegranate molasses
rose water
verjus

SPIRITS
Goldwasser
rose grappa

COLONIALI
beet powder
cardamom
cloves
Facing Heaven chilies (any chili
    will do but I love that name)
bitter chocolate–Venezuelan Black
    100% cacao chocolate
cinnamon
coriander
(Mexican) chocolate powder
fennel
ginger
grains of paradise
green peppercorns
nutmeg
pink peppercorns
Bartolomeo Scappi's spice mix
Szechuan peppercorns
pomegranate seeds
sumac

BASIC PROCEDURES & PREPARATIONS

This section outlines the basic techniques used to prepare hundreds of classic preparations. Combine these simple procedures with the ingredients featured in the earlier larder lists to build your own mental larder. Use ingredients as a writer uses words and an artist uses paints to create your own flavors and dishes. Just like colors are mixed, understand the classic combinations and techniques outlined in this section so you can Jackson Pollock with confidence.

FLAVOR BOMBS

Believe it or not, I am going to teach you how to make a BOMB! Specifically a FLAVOR BOMB! Yes, the following recipes describe the process of mixing explosive flavors with detonating tastes that ambush the taste buds with dangerously delicious results. For years I have been plotting to extract and combine power-packed glutamates with igniting inosinates to build The U (for umami)-BOMB, the ultimate taste explosion and a culinary force to be reckoned with. A word of warning: umami and the building of flavor bombs is all about balance, and not about how many anchovies can you fit on a teaspoon. Control your explosions to be precise and effective. Bombs away!

Whipping it up

Could anything be more magical than the beating
of oil into egg yolk to produce that most sublime–
and useful–of sauces, mayonnaise? Well, yes …
even more magical is the way basic mayonnaise can
be transformed by making simple changes or additions.
Obvious examples are the basic pink cocktail sauce
served with shrimp and avocado achieved by the
addition of tomato ketchup, brandy, Worcestershire
sauce, and a pinch of paprika. Wonder of wonders,
that again can become thousand-island dressing
when other ingredients, such as chopped onion
and red bell peppers, are added.

Basic mayonnaise can be made either by hand
or in a food processor. Either way, both the egg yolks
and olive oil should be at room temperature. Some
recommend adding a teaspoon of mustard to help
emulsify the egg yolk in the oil. Others use a blend
of peanut and olive oils for a more delicate flavor and
color: start with the olive oil and end with a good-
quality vegetable oil. I just grab what's to hand.
I only make my own homemade mayo to accompany
poached fish and shellfish. For the transformations
opposite, I use a good-quality commercial mayonnaise,
like Hellmann's, as, apart from the time saved,
the result is a lot lighter.

15th July 2009

conny jude©2009

1 BASIC MAYONNAISE

2 egg yolks
1 cup light olive oil
lemon juice
salt

1 Place the egg yolks in a clean bowl or processor and begin to whisk vigorously–always in the same direction.
2 While whisking, pour a steady but very fine and continuous stream of olive oil into the eggs. DO NOT STOP WHISKING AS THIS POINT IS MAKE OR BREAK! As the eggs absorb the oil, the mixture will thicken.
3 When the mayonnaise is ready (holding a shape), season to taste with lemon juice and salt.

NOTES If the oil is added too quickly, the eggs will separate. Do not persist in flogging a 'dead' egg; it'll never come round. Start afresh in a clean bowl with just one egg yolk. Once sure the oil has taken and the mayonnaise is forming, you can then steadily add the separated mixture in a slow stream while still whisking vigorously in one direction. Continue adding oil until you have the quantity you need.

TASTY TRANSFORMATIONS

Simply add the ingredients listed below to 1 cup of mayonnaise and blend in a processor until smooth and tasty. In sauces like this there is really no need for quantities; I have put them here as a guideline but let your taste buds guide you. Remember that commercial mayonnaise is already well seasoned, so don't add salt or pepper until the very end.

2 PINK COCKTAIL (MARIE ROSE) SAUCE

Adapt this for shrimp cocktail using shredded iceberg lettuce. Or try hanging juicy cooked chilled Mediterranean shrimp like synchronized swimmers around a bowl filled with crushed ice and some of this sauce set in the middle. Traditionally lightly whipped cream was added to this sauce for an even more delicate color and texture. Try adding a little cream and a drop of rose water. I also then like to decorate it with rose and pink pepper gold dust (see page 39).
3 tablespoons tomato ketchup
1 tablespoon Worcestershire sauce
1 tablespoon Cognac
1 tablespoon sherry
dash of Tabasco sauce
lemon juice
pinch of paprika

This sauce has to be a delicate pale pink. Adjust the color by adding more mayonnaise or ketchup accordingly.

3 TONNATA SAUCE

This sauce is traditionally served with sliced cold veal in a dish known as *vitello tonnato*. It is also delicious with any cold white meat, fish, or cooked eggs.
3½ ounces canned tuna in olive oil, drained
yolks of 2 hard-cooked eggs
2 anchovy fillets in olive oil, drained
1 tablespoon capers in vinegar, drained
3 gherkins
lemon juice
salt
white pepper
Process the tuna, egg yolks, anchovies, capers. and gherkins with 1 cup ready-made mayonnaise as above until smooth. Then let down to a soft (but not runny) spreadable consistency with lemon juice and season with salt and white pepper.

4 TARTARE SAUCE

This sauce goes hand in hand with fried fish and seafood.
1 tablespoon chopped gherkins
1 tablespoon chopped rinsed and drained capers
1 tablespoon chopped fresh flat-leaf parsley
1 tablespoon chopped fresh tarragon
1 tablespoon chopped fresh chervil or dill
yolks of 2 hard-cooked eggs
1 tablespoon finely chopped onion (optional, I hate onion breath!)
1 teaspoon mustard
salt and freshly ground pepper

5 ORANGE MAYONNAISE

This is delicious with cold poached asparagus.
grated zest and juice of ½ orange (preferably a blood orange)
dash of Tabasco sauce
lemon juice
dash of Grand Marnier (optional)
Adjust the consistency until right for your use, adding more orange juice, if necessary.

6 AGLIATA

This garlic mayonnaise, also known as aïoli, is to vampires what meat is to vegetarians.
4 large garlic cloves
salt and freshly ground pepper
lemon juice
Crush the garlic with a teaspoon of sea salt to a paste, then add the mayonnaise and season.

7 CARPACCIO SAUCE

The classic Harry's Bar condiment (see page 61).
2–3 teaspoons Worcestershire sauce
lemon juice
1 teaspoon Dijon mustard
splash of brandy
3 tablespoons milk
salt and white pepper
Mix the Worcestershire sauce, lemon juice, mustard, brandy, and mayonnaise. Add just enough milk to lengthen the sauce so that it just coats the back of a spoon. Season to taste.

Hey pesto!

The word *pestare* means 'to pound' in Italian, hence 'pesto' and 'pestle' and mortar. Although a food processor can be used, smaller quantities are just as quickly dealt with using a pestle and mortar—with only two things to wash up. The weight of the pestle literally crushes the ingredients, causing them to bruise and release all their depth and density. It gets to the essence of all things bashed. A pestle and mortar with a rough interior such as granite gives the best results as it helps in the bashing process to break things down.

For transformations more precious than the sum of their parts, it is always preferable to buy the best-quality ingredients you can afford, especially in these simple pesto and salsa recipes that rely heavily on the characteristics of their ingredients.

Aside from dressing pasta, pesto can be used as a flavor bomb in soups and stews. It can also be combined with equal amounts of bread crumbs for a tasty crust or crumb, mixed with cream cheese for a simple dip or served plain on bruschetta.

1 BASIC BASIL PESTO

2 large handfuls of fresh basil
(leaves only)
1–2 garlic cloves
1–2 tablespoons pine nuts, toasted
in a dry pan
sea salt and freshly ground
black pepper
1 ounce pecorino cheese, grated
1 ounce Parmesan cheese, grated
extra virgin olive oil

1 Place the basil leaves in a stone mortar together with the garlic, toasted pine nuts, and a pinch of sea salt. Crush the ingredients to release their flavors, taking care not to be rough as this will spoil the texture of the finished pesto.
2 Add the cheeses.
3 Pour in a fine steady stream of oil, stirring until you reach your chosen consistency (depending on what you are using it for). Adjust the seasoning.

NOTES A more delicate and perhaps more 'naïve' pesto can be achieved without the cheese and pine nuts. For Creamy pesto pasta or vegetable dressing, mix equal quantities of the Basic pesto and heavy cream, and heat through gently.

TASTY TRANSFORMATIONS

In all these recipes you are aiming for a balance of flavors where no one ingredient predominates. Taste as you go.

2 ARUGULA, MINT & PISTACHIO

This makes a refreshing alternative to classic basil pesto.
1 small handful of fresh mint leaves
1 handful of fresh arugula leaves
½ cup roasted pistachio nuts
1–2 garlic cloves
¼ ounce grated Parmesan cheese
grated zest and squeeze of juice
from a lemon
olive oil
salt and freshly ground
black pepper

3 MIXED HERBS, LEMON & ANCHOVY

This is also a favorite– too delicious for words!
2 handfuls of your favorite
fresh herbs
2 anchovies in oil, drained
grated zest and squeeze of juice
from a lemon
good extra virgin olive oil
Anchovies can be omitted and a couple of toasted walnuts and a few black olives can be added to make it truly U-mamma!: leave anchovies in for double U-mamma pesto!

4 PEANUT, CHILI, CILANTRO & SESAME

This is delicious with Oriental noodles and stir-fried shrimp, chicken, or beef. I like to decorate it with Furikake Stardust (see page 39) and Food Bling (see page 40).
handful of fresh cilantro
handful of fresh sweet Oriental basil
1 tablespoon unsalted roasted
peanuts
1 red or green Thai chili,
finely chopped
sesame oil
dash of soy sauce
grated zest and juice of a lime
½ teaspoon honey
2 teaspoons grated fresh gingerroot
salt

5 ROSE CHERMOULA

This is based on *chermoula*, the North African condiment. Italy has a checkered political history in that part of the world, and it is where Bettino Craxi, the 66th Italian prime minister, fled to avoid a jail sentence. Fortunately, taste is nonpolitical and these heady ingredients have crossed borders forever. Celebrate them in this most magical of sauces without looking for your passport. It is my personal favorite in this group. Serve it on grilled white meat and fish and shellfish.

4 garlic cloves
1 teaspoon coriander seeds
3 heaped teaspoons ground cumin seeds
1 teaspoon fennel seeds
salt flakes and freshly ground
black pepper
2 large handfuls of fresh flat-leaf
parsley, chopped
1 large handful of fresh dill, chopped
3 teaspoons rose petals
⅔ cup extra virgin olive oil
4 tablespoons lemon juice
splash of Tabasco sauce
Pound the garlic, seeds, and a couple of pinches of salt flakes into a paste. Add the parsley, dill, and rose petals, and continue to pound. Gradually add oil and lemon juice to produce a consistency somewhere between a pesto and a dressing. Season with Tabasco and more salt and pepper to taste.

6 CHIMICHURRI

This is my version of the Argentinian marinade/sauce for grilled meat. Do you know how many Italians live in Argentina?!
½ bunch of fresh flat-leaf parsley
½ bunch of fresh cilantro
8 garlic cloves, roughly chopped
¾ cup extra virgin olive oil
4 tablespoons red wine vinegar
juice of ½ lemon
½ red onion, roughly chopped
salt flakes and freshly ground
black pepper
Blend all the ingredients together and season to taste.

7 TAPENADE

Drive along the Italian Riviera where the Taggiasche olives come from and see how quickly it becomes French. *Vive la Difference!* This sauce is delicious on toasted country-style bread, cooked eggs or as a dip for crudités.
½ pound pitted black olives
(Taggiasche/Kalamata)
7 ounces capers, rinsed and drained
2½ ounces tuna in olive oil, drained
3½ ounces anchovy fillets in oil,
rinsed and drained
1 teaspoon Dijon mustard
1–2 garlic cloves
a good glug (about ½ cup) olive oil
dash of Cognac
sprig of fresh thyme
freshly ground black pepper
juice of ½ lemon
Pound or blend the olives, capers, tuna, and anchovies with the mustard and garlic. When reduced to a paste, gradually add the oil, stirring vigorously until a thick 'pesto' consistency is reached. Add a dash of Cognac, a little chopped thyme, generous grindings of black pepper, and lemon juice to taste.

Chopping & changing

This section is all about cutting it in the kitchen and deals with the diced and finely chopped. All the ingredients in this section are transformed by using a sharp knife or blade. Forget fancy knife work, unless it is a skill you do really possess–slowly and safely does it. You do not want any additional and unwanted flavors in your food!

Mixtures of chopped vegetables and/or herbs are at the heart of many Italian dishes, from the classic *soffritto* that forms the flavoring base of many soups, stews, and sauces to the tasty *gremolata* sprinkled over veal and seafood dishes, as well as the wide range of salsas or relishes to accompany so many foods.

Ideal for quickly transforming simply grilled meat or fish, salsas and relishes are quick to prepare and always impress. Try serving the Strawberry, cucumber and cilantro salsa with the Seared carpaccio on page 121, with or without the Rose horseradish. Another personal favorite is grilled tuna steaks with Mango, mint, grappa, and lime salsa, which is literally cooked in minutes.

For best results, cover and leave the salsas to stand for half an hour to an hour in the refrigerator before serving. This allows the juices to be released and the flavors to mingle. If you don't have time, though, keep your guests chatting for an extra minute or two.

1 BASIC SALSA ROSSA

Try this on top of veal Milanese or any of its transformations.

½ pound whole tomatoes, chopped (skins and seeds included)
1 ounce fresh wild arugula leaves, torn
10g fresh basil leaves, torn
2 tablespoons extra virgin olive oil
drizzle of balsamic vinegar
salt flakes and freshly ground black pepper

Chop the ingredients into small, fingernail-sized cubes and mix.

NOTE For a Salsa Rossa Piccante to serve with grilled sausages, omit the arugula and add ⅓ ounce each rinsed, drained and chopped capers and chopped, pitted black olives, 1–2 finely chopped anchovy fillets, and the juice and grated zest of 1 lemon.

TASTY TRANSFORMATIONS

2 SALSA VERDE

Another classic pounded sauce is salsa verde, a 'green' sauce that is traditionally served with grilled fish, boiled meats, etc. It makes a valuable addition to any repertoire. The ingredients for this sauce can also be pounded, so it possibly sits on the fence between pounded and chopped. I usually blend them on the pulse setting of the food processor, so that it does not go to mush.

5 large sprigs of fresh flat-leaf parsley
4 anchovy fillets in oil, well drained (optional)
2 garlic cloves
3 ounces pickled gherkins
3 ounces capers, rinsed and drained
¾ ounce fresh celery leaves
3 tablespoons extra virgin olive oil
dash of white-wine vinegar
salt flakes and freshly ground black pepper

3 STRAWBERRY, CUCUMBER, & CILANTRO SALSA

An added sprinkling of Rose stardust (see page 39) brings out the true magic of this salsa, which is delicious with grilled red meats and robust fish.

5 ounces strawberries, chopped
3 ounces cucumber, chopped
2 ounces red onion, chopped
¼ ounce fresh cilantro, chopped

¼ ounce fresh mint, chopped
juice of 2 limes
3 tablespoons extra virgin olive oil
salt flakes and freshly ground black pepper

4 PINK GRAPEFRUIT, FENNEL, & POMEGRANATE RELISH

This works well with duck breast and other fattier grills.

3 ounces fennel, chopped
3 ounces pink grapefruit segments, chopped
2 ounces pomegranate seeds
¼ ounce red onion, chopped
3 tablespoons extra virgin olive oil
juice of ½ lemon
1 teaspoon Rose stardust (optional, page 39)
salt flakes and freshly ground black pepper

5 WHOLE LEMON RELISH

Although unlike the other transformations, I have to include this recipe, given to me by Gillian Riley, whose vast historical knowledge and up-to-date passion for food combine to create recipes that are both rooted and spirited. This relish, containing nothing but lemons, sugar, and salt, is neither sweet nor salty, but a tangy, refreshing relish bursting with flavors that work so well with fish. Not that it needs it, but for even more

flavor, bomb this relish with Rose stardust (see page 39); it not only looks beautiful but adds a spicy headiness.

2 whole unwaxed lemons
unrefined superfine sugar
salt flakes

Thinly slice the lemons into rounds–zest, pulp, and all. Chop these into tiny fingernail-sized pieces. Discard the pips and season with a balance of sugar and salt. This relish is neither sweet nor salty, but a tangy and refreshing condiment that is quite delicious with fish.

6 CHILI SHRIMP RELISH

Use as a vegetable soup and risotto topping (see pages 68–72).

14 ounces small cooked peeled shrimp (10 ounces for an appetizer)
2 large fresh red chilies, seeded and finely chopped
generous handful of chopped fresh flat-leaf parsley
juice of 2 lemons
salt flakes and freshly ground black pepper

Mix all the ingredients together and marinate/defrost in the refrigerator for a couple of hours.

7 ASPARAGUS & ORANGE SALSA

This salsa goes particularly well with pan-fried duck breast.

5 ounces asparagus stalks, blanched and chopped

¾ ounce Parmesan cheese, coarsely chopped
¾ ounce pitted black olives (Taggiascha or Kalamata), chopped
grated zest and juice of ½ lemon
grated zest and juice of ½ orange
3 tablespoons extra virgin olive oil
salt flakes and freshly ground black pepper

8 EGG & CAPER RELISH

Great with asparagus or artichoke.

3 large hard-cooked eggs (cooked 10 minutes only and immediately cooled to avoid grey-green yolk)
large handful of fresh flat-leaf parsley, chopped
2½ ounces pickled gherkins, chopped
1 ounce capers, roughly chopped
3 tablespoons extra virgin olive oil
1 tablespoon white wine vinegar
grated zest and juice of ½ lemon
3 anchovies in oil, drained and chopped (optional)
salt flakes and freshly ground black pepper

9 MANGO, MINT, GRAPPA, & LIME SALSA

Try this with white crabmeat.

flesh of 2 mangoes, chopped
3 tablespoons extra virgin olive oil
handful of fresh mint leaves
handful of fresh flat-leaf parsley
grated zest and juice of 1 lime
splash of grappa
salt and freshly ground black pepper

The kindest cut

Trifolati (or *al funghetto* as it is know in Liguria) is a way of cooking vegetables in which they are thinly sliced and fried in olive oil with added garlic and parsley. Sometimes a handful of roughly chopped mint and a squeeze of lemon juice are also added. Once you've got the hang of this incredibly easy method, you will be able to apply it across a wide range of ingredients. Zucchini, mushrooms, Jerusalem artichokes, eggplants and potatoes lend themselves best to this treatment.

The versatility of this simple cooking method is endless: stir trifolati through pastas and risotti, use as a topping for Beef tagliata (see page 125) and other grilled meats and fish. Trifolati also make tasty side orders or simple antipasti on top of crostini. A mutation of this dish is *a scapece*, a sweet-and-sour Sicilian dish in which vegetables or fish are deep-fried instead of sautéed and dressed with a splash of vinegar, chopped mint, salt, and pepper.

1 BASIC ZUCCHINI TRIFOLATA

4 tablespoons extra virgin olive oil
3 garlic cloves, halved lengthways
8 zucchini, sliced across into
    ½-inch rounds
generous handful of fresh flat-leaf
    parsley, chopped
salt flakes and freshly ground
    black pepper
(fresh or dried chili can be added
    to this dish for a more
    piquant flavor)

1 Heat the oil in a deep frying pan that has a lid over a moderate to high heat. Add the garlic.
2 When sizzling, add the zucchini. Season and cook for about 5 minutes, stirring to make sure all the slices are coated and lightly browned.
3 Add the parsley, cover, and finish cooking on a very low heat. The cooking time from beginning to end should be about 10–15 minutes.

TASTY TRANSFORMATIONS

2 ZUCCHINI, PRAWN, & SAFFRON

This goes well with tagliatelle.
5 ounces raw king prawns, shelled
    and deveined
generous splash of heavy cream
pinch of saffron stems
Halve the basic recipe and cut the zucchini into half-moons. Heat the oil and sizzle the garlic, then add the prawns with the zucchini. Continue as for the basic recipe. When the prawns are cooked and the zucchini lightly colored, add the cream and saffron. Stir well. Season and cook on a high heat until the sauce has a coating consistency.

3 ARTICHOKE, PROSCIUTTO, LEMON, & RICOTTA

Serve this with pasta, topped with crumbled ricotta and mixed chopped parsley and mint.
2 ounces prosciutto, chopped
2 pounds baby artichokes
grated zest and squeeze of juice
    from 1 lemon
splash of heavy cream
Halve the basic recipe and sauté the prosciutto until crisp. Add this with the artichokes and proceed as the basic recipe. When cooked, add the lemon zest and juice with the cream.

4 ASPARAGUS, ANCHOVY, AND/ OR ALMOND WITH BITTER ORANGE

Use as a soup topping or a pasta stir-through.
2 pounds asparagus, roughly chopped
2 anchovy fillets, drained and
    chopped, and/or a handful
    of scorched flaked almonds
grated zest and squeeze of juice
    from 1 orange
Replace the zucchini with asparagus and add the extra ingredients.

5 SWEET-AND-SOUR CARROTS WITH HONEY & THYME

This makes a lovely side dish with almost anything, as do all the following recipes.
2 pounds carrots, thinly sliced
2 tablespoons runny honey
1 tablespoon vinegar (wine or
    everyday balsamic)
3 sprigs of fresh thyme, leaves only
Follow the basic recipe, replacing the zucchini with carrots and adding the additional ingredients.

6 MUSHROOM TRIFOLATA

Serve this on top of a grilled Beef tagliata (see page 125), stirred through pasta as is or with cream, or simply on crostini.

2 pounds porcini (cèpe) or
    portobello mushrooms
4 tablespoons extra virgin olive oil
3 garlic cloves, halved lengthways
splash of white wine (optional)
generous handful of fresh flat-leaf
    parsley, chopped
salt flakes and freshly ground
    black pepper
1 or 2 tablespoons of butter
    (optional)
Cut the mushrooms into ½-inch thick slices. Heat the oil and cook with the garlic as above. Once the mushrooms have released all their liquid and this has evaporated, splash with the wine if using. Once any wine has evaporated, add the parsley, season, and continue to cook until the mushrooms are soft but still whole. Stir in the butter.
NOTE For a mushroom and truffle trifolata, add a few drops of truffle oil.

7 ARTICHOKE TRIFOLATA

2 pounds baby artichokes
3 garlic cloves, halved lengthways
4 tablespoons extra virgin olive oil
generous handful of flat-leaf
    parsley, chopped
Remove the artichokes' tough outer leaves. Cut in half and scoop out the hairy chokes with the point of a knife. As you prepare each one, drop it in a bowl of cold water with the juice of ½ lemon (leave the squeezed lemon in the water). Leave to soak for about 20 minutes to prevent discoloration. Drain and rinse well. Cut in ¼-inch slices. Heat the oil and garlic, and proceed as for zucchini.
NOTE I like to add lemon juice and mint to artichoke trifolata.

8 POTATO TRIFOLATA

2 pounds large potatoes
3 garlic cloves, halved lengthways
4 tablespoons extra virgin olive oil
generous handful of fresh flat-leaf
    parsley, chopped
Slice the potatoes into ¼-inch-thick rounds. Heat the oil and garlic, and proceed as for the zucchini. If the potatoes are sticking, add a tiny splash of water before covering with the lid. Stir frequently.
NOTES: This potato mix is delicious prepared in a large ovenproof frying pan and, when the potato slices are cooked but still al dente, add 7 ounces mascarpone and a generous handful of grated Parmesan, with salt and black pepper to taste. Toss all together and put in a hot oven to crisp up, topped with little dabs of butter and a sprinkling of coarsely chopped sage leaves. I have also done this dish with a little less Parmesan and a sprinkling of Wild mushroom and anchovy stardust (see page 39).

Compound interest

My butter mixes have melted the hearts of many a hardened foodie, especially when I have added a teaspoon of edible gold or silver flakes to the mixture (see page 40). As the butter melts, the meat is seductively gilded with mouthwatering flavors, exotic colors, and glistering precious metals. For extra effect and texture, I use a Stardust blend (see page 39), coarse for visuals and finely ground for color and flavor. Since all these butters freeze well, it is worth making a double batch: one for the refrigerator and one for the freezer. Once you get the hang of it, you can beat almost anything, from curry to caviar, into a compound butter. Similar preparations can be made with creamy cheeses, such as Gorgonzola and mascarpone, instead of butter.

1 BASIC MAÎTRE D'HÔTEL BUTTER

Use coin-shaped slices to top grilled meats and fish.

3½ ounces softened salted butter
1 tablespoon chopped fresh flat-leaf parsley
grated zest of 1 lemon and squeeze of juice
salt flakes and freshly ground black pepper

In a bowl, cream the butter with the other ingredients. Adjust the seasoning and roll the mixture into a sausage shape. Wrap in plastic and chill in the refrigerator until firm.

TASTY TRANSFORMATIONS

2 GARLIC BUTTER

Ideal on crostini or traditional garlic bread.
Simply add 3 crushed garlic cloves to the basic mixture.

3 U-MAMMA! BUTTER

This goes with anything.
3½ ounces softened butter
1 tablespoon Wild mushroom and anchovy stardust (page 39)
½ tablespoon finely grated Parmesan (optional)
freshly ground black pepper

4 HORSERADISH & ROSE BUTTER

Delicious with grilled red meat and oily fish.
3½ ounces softened butter
1 tablespoon Rose stardust (page 39)
2 ounces grated fresh horseradish

5 CHOCOLATE & CHILI BUTTER

Use with game and legumes or even on a bread-and-butter pudding made with hot cross buns.
3½ ounces softened butter
1 tablespoon Chocolate chili stardust (page 39)
grated zest of 1 orange

6 BAROLO BUTTER

This is my favorite compound butter, not least because of its crimson hue. It is ideal with red meat.
2 banana shallots, finely chopped
sprig of fresh thyme, leaves only
1 cup Barolo wine
½ cup softened salted butter
Sweat the chopped shallots and thyme leaves in a dry saucepan over a low heat until soft, about 10 minutes, making sure it does not burn. When soft and beginning to caramelize, add the wine and reduce over a medium heat until there is no liquid left. Leave to cool. When cool, cream together with the butter until a uniform crimson color. Roll and refrigerate as in the basic recipe.

7 PINOT GRIGIO BUTTER

Ideal with white meats and fish.
In the previous transformation, replace the Barolo with Pinot Grigio and the thyme with tarragon.

8 BURNT WALNUT & GORGONZOLA CHEESE

Try it. You'll soon know what to use it with!
5 ounces Gorgonzola Piccante
2½ ounces toasted walnuts, chopped
drop or two of port (optional)
freshly ground black pepper

9 LEMON MASCARPONE CHEESE

Use as a creamy alternative to butter on vegetable dishes or anywhere.
4 ounces mascarpone cheese
grated zest of 2 lemons and 1 teaspoon juice
salt flakes and freshly ground black pepper
Combine all the ingredients. A pinch of Rose stardust (see page 39) is wonderful in this zesty mix.

Love me tender

Marinades exist to both tenderize and flavor. In some cases they are used and then discarded; in others they double up as a tasty baste or even as sauce. In stews they are part of the fabric of the dish and slow-cooked with the meat until the very end. Remember that marinades that don't get incorporated and cooked with the dish may contain raw meat or fish juices that could contain unwanted nasties and should not be consumed raw. This also means that this sort of marinade, once used, cannot be stored and used again unless it is cooked.

1 BASIC RED WINE MARINADE

This is ideal for most red meats and game.

NOTE If you are not incorporating the marinade in the dish, as in a stew, the amounts given can be halved. If the resulting marinade doesn't quite cover the meat, then turn it regularly in the liquid or put everything in a stout food bag and exclude as much air as possible before sealing it and shake it well from time to time.

2 carrots, cut in chunks
2 onions, cut in chunks
2 celery ribs, cut in chunks
3 garlic cloves, crushed
2 sprigs of fresh thyme
2 bay leaves
1 teaspoon salt flakes
2 teaspoons black peppercorns
1 bottle of red wine
1¼ cups olive oil
2 cups red wine vinegar
(leave out if marinade is for a stew where liquid will be used)

Mix everything together well and add the meat to be marinated, ensuring it is fully immersed in the liquid (if not enough, increase the quantities). Leave to marinate for up to 12 hours in a cool place.

VARIATION For a Basic White Wine Marinade ideal for white meats and fish, use a dry white wine instead of a red, omit the vinegar, and replace the carrots, celery, and garlic with the grated zest and juice of 1 lemon and the thyme, with a handful of flat-leaf parsley, roughly torn. Leave to marinate in the refrigerator.

TASTY TRANSFORMATIONS

2 MYRTLE, JUNIPER, & GRAPPA MARINADE

This is ideal for game.
1 bottle of red wine
balsamic instead of red wine vinegar
4 teaspoon juniper berries
½ handful of myrtle leaves
3 cloves
generous splash of grappa or gin
NOTE Juniper berries can be replaced with a tablespoon of Lavender stardust (see page 39).

3 ORANGE, ANCHOVY, & CINNAMON MARINADE

Ideal for game birds.
1 bottle of red wine
1 cinnamon stick or 1 tablespoon Renaissance stardust (page 39)
peel of 1 orange
3 salted anchovies (optional)

4 RED U-MAMMA! MARINADE

Use for red meat and meaty fish.
1 bottle of red wine
3 tablespoons balsamic syrup instead of the red wine vinegar
3 anchovies in oil, drained
handful of dried porcini (cèpe) mushrooms
drizzle of truffle oil
splash of Worcestershire sauce

5 POMEGRANATE, ROSE, & MINT MARINADE

Lovely with quail or white meat, or even robust fish or shellfish.
1 bottle of white wine
2 cups unsweetened pomegranate juice
generous handful of mint leaves, roughly torn
1 tablespoon pomegranate molasses
3 limes, 2 chopped and pips removed, plus the juice of the third
1 tablespoon Rose stardust (page 39) or a sprinkling of dried edible rose petals

6 ROSEMARY, APPLE, & LAVENDER MARINADE

Use with pork and veal.
1 bottle of white wine
3 sprigs of fresh rosemary
pinch of lavender flowers
1 tablespoon Lavender stardust (page 39) or a sprinkling of dried edible lavender
1¼ cups unsweetened apple juice or 1 tablespoon runny honey
finely chopped peel of 1 apple

7 WHITE U-MAMMA! MARINADE

Use with any white meat or fish. Mix three equal measures of white wine, olive oil, and soy sauce, add the remaining ingredients for the base except, of course, the wine, oil, and vinegar, plus the following:
3 anchovies in oil, drained and roughly chopped
handful of pitted green olives in oil, drained and roughly chopped
1 lime, chopped
1 large chunk of gingerroot, grated

8 MOCHA CHILI BARBECUE MARINADE

This mix can be used as a marinade or a finishing sauce. It is ideal for ribs (see page 148), wings, or sausages
½ cup strong espresso coffee
½ cup balsamic vinegar
½ cup runny honey
1 cup tomato ketchup
2 tablespoons Dijon mustard
2 tablespoons ground cumin
1 tablespoon grated 100% cacao
1 teaspoon chili flakes (or more if looking for real heat)
1 tablespoon Worcestershire sauce
Mix all the ingredients together in a small heavy-based pan with a tablespoon of water. Bring to a boil over a high heat. Turn heat right down and let simmer for 15–20 minutes. Leave to cool completely, then blend.

Rubbing it in

Unsurprisingly, meat responds to aromatic massage with flavoring ingredients. Some people actually refer to these, very sensibly, as 'dry marinades'. Tougher cuts can be made into noble dishes when rubbed with one of my Stardust Rubs. These stardusts are pure magic and make ideal seasonings for all sorts of foods. You can rub them into meat, poultry, fish, etc. that has been brushed with oil before grilling or roasting, etc. and/or use them as a seasoning garnish/condiment after cooking. Use a coffee grinder for fine powders and a pestle and mortar for a less refined finish.

I rub into most things–it works particularly well on roast chicken and ribs (see page 148). Remember, though, that rubs are not to be eaten raw and, because of their very strong flavors, should only be used to season things that are going to be heated to a high temperature.

I have gathered and milled the stars for you;
And danced them to your lips;
Eat slowly, lest you should swallow me whole
and forget to spit out the pips!

1 BASIC WET RUB

1 onion, peeled and quartered
bunch of fresh rosemary, leaves only
bunch of fresh sage, leaves only
handful of fresh flat-leaf parsley
2 garlic cloves
Aromat or salt flakes and
*   freshly ground black pepper*
olive oil

1 Place all the ingredients except the seasoning in a food processor with a little olive oil and pulse until chopped into little pieces–not a pulp.
2 Add more oil to make a runny paste.
3 Season to taste. If you are MSG-sensitive, use salt instead of Aromat, but know that you are losing some umami. (You could always try adding a couple of anchovies to boost the U-Factor.)

VARIATION For a sunny Mediterranean twist, add a generous handful of pitted green olives, the juice and zest of a lemon, and a tablespoon of fennel seeds.

TASTY TRANSFORMATIONS

2 DRY RUBS

Coarsely mill the following mixtures to create flavorful rubs ideal for roasting or grilling meats and robust fish and shellfish.

3 WET RUBS

These even coarser rubs are for grilling and roasting where you want to give meat or fish a crust that can be brushed off to serve. Using a pestle and mortar, coarsely pound the ingredients, adding olive oil, garlic, and a handful of appropriate herbs.
VARIATION The juice and zest of an orange, lemon, or lime can be added to these mixtures, as can a splash of grappa, gin, brandy, etc.

4 STARDUSTS

These are finely milled to a powder to create decorative tasty sprinkles.

5 RENAISSANCE RUB/STARDUST

Try this with white meats and fish.
2 cinnamon sticks
1 level tablespoon salt flakes
2 tablespoons granulated unrefined
*   cane sugar*
In a small coffee grinder, blend all the ingredients to a fine dust.
VARIATION I like to add a pinch each of silver and gold dust (see page 40) for extra sparkly magic.

6 ROSE RUB/ STARDUST

This goes well with lamb, chicken, game, beef, fish, and shellfish. It is also amazing on sliced avocado with olive oil and a twist of lime! I also add gold flakes (see page 40) for a truly beautiful effect.
1 tablespoon dried rose petals
1 teaspoon bay rose pink peppercorns
pinch of sumac
1 teaspoon salt flakes

7 WILD MUSHROOM & ANCHOVY RUB/STARDUST

This goes with anything savory.
¼ ounce dried mixed wild mushrooms
¼ ounce dried anchovy powder (see below)
To dry anchovies you need a jar or can of salted anchovies in oil. Preheat a very cool oven (215°F). Lay out the drained anchovy fillets on a baking tray. Place in the oven, lower the heat to 175°F or the lowest it will go, and leave for about 1 hour, until dried. Drain off any excess oil halfway through the process and return to the oven to finish off. You can speed the process up by gently spreading the fillets with a fork while draining. Anchovies dried in this way will keep in a sealed container in the refrigerator for 3 days. Grind them to a powder using a pestle and mortar.

8 LAVENDER RUB/STARDUST

Lovely with pork, veal, and spring lamb.
¼ ounce dried anchovy powder (see previous transformation)
1 teaspoon lavender
1 teaspoon dried green peppercorns
5 teaspoons dried rosemary
2 teaspoons juniper berries

9 CHOCOLATE CHILI RUB/ STARDUST

This is sensational with red meats and ribs.
½ ounce 100% cacao dark chocolate
1 teaspoon dried chili flakes
2 long strips of orange zest
½ teaspoon Mexican cacao powder
Dry the orange zest on a baking tray in a cool oven, until crisp but not burned. Blend with the other ingredients.
VARIATION I love to add gold flakes (see page 40) to this blend for Inca mystery.

10 FURIKAKE RUB/STARDUST

Furry Car Key! This is a really tasty Japanese blend and, although not strictly Italian, I have used enough of it to make it so. Ready-blended *furikio*–which now has a whole new meaning for those of you who speak Italian!– can now be bought from any good Japanese food store.

I like to mix it with gold flakes for an extra-special decoration.
1 ounce white sesame seeds
1 ounce black sesame seeds
1 sheet of nori seaweed, blended into flakes
1 tablespoon ground red shiso leaves (optional)

11 COFFEE CARDAMOM RUB/ STARDUST

This goes well with most red meats.
4 teaspoons black peppercorns
2 tablespoons coffee beans
3 cardamom pods
⅓ teaspoon salt flakes
¼ teaspoon brown sugar

12 BLACKENED RUB/STARDUST

This is loosely based on a Cajun seasoning mix and is really great with anything.
4 ounces paprika
2½ ounces salt
2½ ounces ground white pepper (freshly ground is best)
2½ ounces garlic powder
2½ ounces onion powder
2½ tablespoons dried thyme
2½ tablespoons dried oregano
2½ tablespoons cayenne pepper
2½ tablespoons freshly ground black pepper

Food bling: edible noble metals

'Food bling' is my term for edible noble metals, namely gold and silver. Although the practice of eating gold and silver leaf was most recently fashionable in the 1980s, it can be traced to as far back as 13BC. Indeed, it was the alchemic scholars of ancient Egypt and Persia who first put their money where their mouths were as they experimented with the golden game of alchemy and the transformation of base metals into gold. The ingestion of gold was seen to give the light from the sun and higher powers, and considered a potential fast track to immortality. To this end a potion containing liquid gold was distilled and heralded as the elixir of life.

In truth, alchemy was just a shiny metaphor for a more profound personal transformation, and those seeking spiritual enlightenment at a time where it was not permitted, hid behind the cloak of science in order to pursue the light. The sun became gold, the moon became silver, and the men and women became whole through the pursuit of knowledge in the magnum opus of their life's journey.

It is ironic that the last time we put our money where our mouths were was in the greedy 1980s, when the pursuit of enlightenment was an arduous task in a world busy pursuing the promise of eternal wealth.

Somewhat perversely, edible gold and silver became glaring mascots for a 'gilt'-free society, and delicacies such as gilded sushi became the elixir of life in the fast lane, swallowed without a hint of irony or reflection.

Today it is more than apparent that Shakespeare was right: 'All that glisters is not gold'. I use smatterings of gold and silver beacons in my food in celebration that we are moving forward to a time when the pursuit of enlightenment will once again be considered noble. Enchanting and optimistic, these shiny flakes connect us to the earth, and all the knowledge stored within her core.

NOTE Edible gold and silver are sold in various forms: dust, flakes, and leaf. Ensure that your product has been approved for food standards and ask to see certification before purchasing. Always use them sparingly as they are not recommended for daily use, but just for adding some magic on special occasions. Both are recognized in Europe and the USA as food colorings, and are used extensively in the liqueur and confectionery industries. Also please read the important note on this subject on page 4.

How will you know your real friends?
Pain is as dear to them as life.
A friend is like gold. Trouble is like fire.
Pure gold delights in the fire.
II, 1458; 1461–RUMI

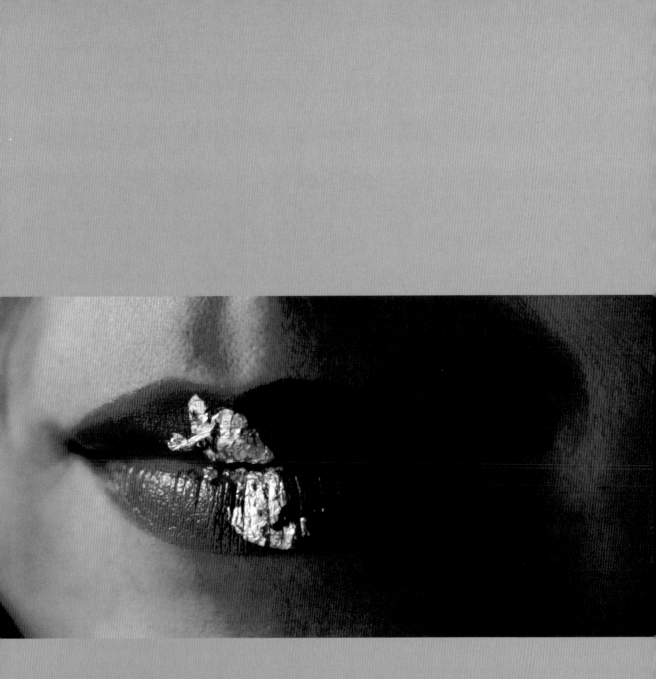

Tasty pastes

These pastes are designed to be concentrated flavor bombs or taste explosions, perfect for taking scratch cooking to another level. Packed with umami, they add instant U-Factor to almost anything. Try bombing everyday dishes, such as stews, soups, risotti, pastas, gravies, and sauces with these intense flavors. I have given some suggestions for good combinations, but please experiment. There are endless possibilities, since there are surprisingly very few flavor boundaries, and you will soon know when you have crossed one!

1 BASIC PARMESAN & PROSCIUTTO PASTE

2¼ ounces lean prosciutto di Parma
1½ ounces Parmigiano Reggiano
    (Parmesan) cheese
2 long strips of lemon zest
3 tablespoons extra virgin olive oil
¼ ounce fresh flat-leaf parsley leaves
splash of warm water to blend

Mix all ingredients using
a hand blender. Store in the
refrigerator, covered in a film of
oil, for up to a week.

NOTES Prosciutto can be
replaced with drained and
rinsed canned white beans.
U-mamma! Bombtastic!
Nuts can also be added to
this mix to make a protein-
packed fix for vegetarians.

TASTY TRANSFORMATIONS

2 BLACK OLIVE, CAPER, & WALNUT PASTE

Makes a lovely addition to pasta
sauces and risotti.

1 ounce toasted walnuts
2½ ounces pitted black olives
    (Taggiasche or Kalamata)
¾ ounce rinsed salted capers
½ garlic clove
1 teaspoon truffle oil

Toast the nuts on a baking tray in
an oven preheated to 350°F until
nicely colored. Remove them
from the oven when they are one
shade before what you want, as
they continue cooking after
leaving the oven. Transfer to a
cold plate to cool. Mix all the
ingredients as above.

3 TOMATO, PEPPER, ORANGE, & CINNAMON PASTE

This is delicious as a topping
for fish soups, like the
Garibaldi's fish soup on page 74.

1 Romano or red bell pepper
1½ ounces concentrated tomato paste
½–1 teaspoon harissa
½ teaspoon ground cinnamon
2 long strips of orange zest
1 anchovy fillet (optional)
1 tablespoon extra virgin olive oil

Bake the pepper in a hot oven
until soft. When cool, skin, and
seed. Proceed as above.

4 GARLIC, SWEET BASIL, & ALMOND PASTE

Great with legumes; see the
lentil soup on page 70.

½ ounce fresh basil, leaves only
pinch of salt flakes
½ garlic clove
1 ounce toasted whole blanched
    almonds
½ teaspoon fennel seeds
grated zest and juice of ½ lemon
1½ tablespoons extra virgin olive
    oil

5 CHILI CHOCOLATE WINE PASTE

This is a very thick paste to
be used in rich stews and game
dishes and is ideal for mixing
with pan juices for a robust and
glossy gravy.

2 ounces ground Venezuelan black
    100% cacao chocolate
½ teaspoon chili flakes
1 tablespoon olive oil
1½ tablespoons full-bodied red wine
½ teaspoon balsamic vinegar DOP
2 teaspoon verjus
½ teaspoon Mexican cacao powder

Blend together, adding more
oil or wine if too thick.

6 PORCINI & TRUFFLE PASTE

Add to meat juices in the pan
with a splash of heavy cream for
a quick sauce, or simply
drop into pastas and risotti.

½ ounce dried porcini mushrooms
truffle oil to blend
salt flakes

Rehydrate the mushrooms as
per instructions. Drain (reserve
the tasty liquid to flavor
something else). Blend with
truffle oil until it forms a thick
paste. Season to taste with salt.

7 TRUFFLE & ANCHOVY PASTE

Ideal for zinging up tomato-
based pasta sauces.

2 jars of anchovies in olive oil
truffle oil to blend

Drain the anchovies and
blend with the truffle oil to
a thick paste.

VARIATION If you are feeling
really extravagant and have
some truffles to hand, this is
delicious with some very fine
truffle shavings in the mixture.

8 ROSE, POMEGRANATE, & MINT PASTE

Tasty and works with anything
from pasta to poultry.

½ ounce fresh mint leaves
zest and juice of ½ lime
1 tablespoon dried rose petals
2 teaspoons dried or fresh
    pomegranate seeds
½ teaspoon pomegranate molasses
1 ounce shelled pistachio nuts
¼ ounce feta cheese
½ teaspoon pink peppercorns
1 tablespoon olive oil
pinch of salt flakes
ground black pepper

Blend everything together,
adding more oil if too thick.

9 ARTICHOKE & BAY PASTE

Great with chicken dishes.

3 ounces artichoke pieces in olive
    oil, drained
2–3 bay leaves
½ garlic clove
1 tablespoon olive oil
pinch of salt flakes
ground black pepper

Blend everything together,
adding more oil if too thick.

Elixirs & potion notions

We are the mirror as well as the face in it
We are tasting the taste this instant of eternity.
We are pain and what cures pain both
We are the sweet cold water
and the jar that pours.
RUMI

The basic recipe, the Black Chocolate Elixir, is actually meant to enhance savory dishes, such as the Beef tagliata on page 125. However, I have also given here some truly sweet sauces to accompany my desserts.

BLACK CHOCOLATE ELIXIR

⅓ cup thick balsamic vinegar
¼ ounce 100% pure cacao (Venezuelan Black), coarsely grated
3 tablespoons extra virgin olive oil

Simply mix all the ingredients together.

TASTY TRANSFORMATIONS

1 TRUFFLE & ANCHOVY ELIXIR

This is delicious on grilled meats and vegetables.
5 tablespoons extra virgin olive oil
2 tablespoons truffle oil
anchovy essence to taste

2 ROSE POMEGRANATE, & GRAPPA ELIXIR

Use this with white fish and meats, and shellfish.
1 tablespoon pomegranate molasses
1 tablespoon grappa
2 drops of rose water
2 tablespoons olive oil
3 cardamom pods, crushed
squeeze of fresh lime juice
salt flakes

3 RED PEPPER & ORANGE OIL

This is perfect with most seafood.
1 cup extra virgin olive oil
4 red bell peppers, roughly chopped, core and seeds removed
2 bay leaves
4 red chilies, 2 left whole and 2 seeded (or both seeded for a milder result)
pinch of saffron strands
peel of 2 oranges
Put a third of the oil in a saucepan with the peppers, chilies, saffron, and bay leaves. Cook over a low heat until the peppers soften. As they soften, add the rest of the oil and the orange peel. Strain and use.

4 OLIVE OR TRUFFLE & GOLD OIL

I like to make my own 'Elixir of Life', or 'Dancing Water' as the Sufi call it, by adding gold flakes to olive oil or truffle oil for pure alchemic drizzle. I use it to dress carpaccios (see page 61) and grilled vegetables.

5 DARK CHOCOLATE DESSERT SAUCE

I have adapted this recipe and the Liquid gold recipe below from culinary wizard Michel Roux Senior's book *Sauces*, which is the culinary Holy Grail and one of my favorites. I have tried and tested hundreds of chocolate sauces over the years, but this one reigns supreme.
3½ ounces chocolate (70% cacao), roughly broken
3½ ounces chocolate (55% cacao), roughly broken
⅔ cup milk
2 tablespoons heavy cream
1 ounce superfine sugar
1 ounce butter
Melt both chocolates in a bowl over a bain-marie. In a saucepan, bring the milk, cream, and sugar to a boil, stirring throughout. Remove from the heat and stir the milk mixture into the chocolate. Return to the pan and heat until it boils again. Remove from the heat and whisk in the butter a little at a time. Pass through a wire mesh sieve. Serve hot.
VARIATIONS Add 1 teaspoon of crushed black peppercorns or chili flakes to this sauce. For an extraordinary transformation, try adding 1 tablespoon thick balsamic vinegar with a high cooked grape must content when whisking in the butter.

6 WHITE CHOCOLATE DESSERT SAUCE

Adapted from *The Ivy Cookbook*, this recipe is to white chocolate what Michel Roux's recipe is to the dark variety.
1¼ pounds white chocolate (chopped)
2¼ cups heavy cream
2 tablespoons condensed milk
Heat the chocolate, cream, and condensed milk together in a bain-marie, stirring occasionally until hot.
VARIATIONS At London's favorite celebrity restaurant, The Ivy, this sauce is served over 'iced berries'. Freeze a selection of small mixed berries going no larger than raspberries and blackberries. Plate about 5 minutes before serving and serve with a jug of the hot sauce. A tablespoon of white balsamic vinegar can be added at the end.

7 SWEET RED FRUIT DESSERT SAUCE

2¼ pounds soft red fruits (strawberries, raspberries, redcurrants, etc.)
confectioners' sugar
Press the berries through a wire sieve and discard the seeds. Sweeten to taste with the confectioners' sugar.
VARIATIONS A squeeze of lemon juice and/or some finely grated lemon zest can be added, as can a pinch of crushed pink or green peppercorns, mint leaves, etc.

8 LIQUID GOLD

I like to make liquid bling by adding a pinch of gold flake (see page 40) to this recipe when it is cool.
11 ounces maple syrup
⅓ cup vodka
Heat the maple syrup until hot but not boiling. Remove from the heat. Stir in the vodka, cover and leave to cool.

Crumbs of comfort

We mistook the full moon for a loaf of bread
and raised our hands to the sky.
RUMI

Superstition says to kiss old bread before discarding,
I say save your kisses for your love and your bread
for the birds. However, yesterday's bread can be part
of tomorrow's banquet, using the recipes opposite.

1 BASIC BREAD CRUMBS

These crumbs can be stored in an airtight container for up to a month. It is therefore worthwhile making a good batch. Be careful using bread with sesame or nut toppings; once crumbed, they are disguised and pose a hidden threat to those with allergies.

2¼ pounds dried white bread (bread can be a couple of days old but not actually stale)

1 Dry the bread out in a low oven to remove all the moisture without coloring it.
2 Blend it in chunks in a food processor until sandy.

NOTE To make a crust from the crumbs for items to be baked, mix equal parts of bread crumbs with any of the pastes on pages 42–3 or pestos on page 28–9. Pack on top of fish, meat or vegetables and top with a small a tablespoon of butter and an extra sprinkling of grated Parmesan cheese before baking. Splash the pan (not the crust) with booze for a saucy tasty mix.

TASTY TRANSFORMATIONS

2 PARMESAN HERB CRUMB

7 ounces dried bread crumbs
2¼ ounces grated Parmesan cheese
1 tablespoon dried oregano
1 teaspoon garlic powder (optional)
grated zest of 1 lemon
salt flakes and freshly ground black pepper

3 BACON, ONION, & SAGE CRUMB

7 ounces dried bread crumbs
2¼ ounces ground cooked smoked bacon (available from supermarkets)
1 tablespoon dried sage
salt flakes and freshly ground black pepper

4 BLACK OLIVE, LEMON, & ANCHOVY CRUMB

7 ounces dried bread crumbs
2 tablespoons Tapenade (page 29)
grated zest of 1 lemon
1 tablespoon dried anchovy powder (page 39)
handful of finely chopped flat-leaf parsley
salt flakes and freshly ground black pepper

5 DRIED WILD MUSHROOM & TARRAGON CRUMB

7 ounces dried bread crumbs
½ ounce powdered wild mushrooms (use a blender)
1 tablespoon dried tarragon
salt flakes and freshly ground black pepper

These delicious stuffings can be used inside birds or rolled into balls and roasted separately. Try the stuffing 'on horseback' by wrapping some in bacon or pancetta. Note that when a bird is stuffed the cooking time needs to be extended.

6 U-MAMMA! STUFFING

1 large Spanish onion, finely chopped
1 garlic clove, very finely chopped
4 tablespoons olive oil,
5 ounces mortadella
5 ounces prosciutto cotto (cooked ham)
1¼ pounds tasty sausage meat
3 ounces Parmesan cheese, grated
2½ ounces pistachio nuts, roughly chopped
3½ ounces dried apricots, roughly chopped
1 large handful of flat-leaf parsley, finely chopped
¼ ounce fresh rosemary leaves, finely chopped
¼ ounce fresh sage leaves, finely chopped
7 ounces dried white bread crumbs (or a handful as needed)

1 whole egg, to bind
salt flakes and freshly ground black pepper

Sauté the onion and garlic in the olive oil until glassy but not colored. Blitz the mortadella and ham in a food processor until finely chopped. Transfer the onion and garlic to a large mixing bowl and add the sausage meat, blitzed mortadella and ham, the Parmesan, pistachio nuts, apricots, herbs, and the egg. Mix together using your hands, adding a fistful of bread crumbs at a time until you reach the desired stuffing consistency. Take care not to over-season this stuffing as it is already umami-packed. I usually add only black pepper. To taste, fry a little of the mixture in the onion pan and assess the seasoning. Do not taste this mixture raw.

7 CHESTNUT STUFFING

1 large Spanish onion, finely chopped
7 ounces bacon, finely chopped
2½ ounces butter
1¾ pounds chestnuts (vacuum-packed cooked and peeled)
7 ounces white bread crumbs
1 whole egg, to bind
1 large handful of fresh flat-leaf parsley, finely chopped
grated zest of 1 lemon
1 teaspoon sugar
salt flakes and freshly ground black pepper

Sauté the onion and bacon in the butter until the onion is glassy but not colored and the bacon is no longer raw. Pulse the chestnuts in a food processor until smooth but with some little chunks. Place the chestnuts and the onion and bacon mixture in a large mixing bowl and, using your hands, squeeze them together, adding the bread crumbs, egg, parsley, lemon zest, and sugar. Season with salt and freshly ground black pepper to taste. If the mixture is too dry, soften with some extra melted butter or another egg.

The Elemental Recipes

Section 2

Nonna Pasqua - in her hotel kitchen.

AIR

'I Was Raw'

Using only truly raw ingredients, the words
'easy' and 'tasty' are taken to a whole new level.
The alchemy is in the combined simplicity.
Obviously, though, the success of every dish
in this section relies heavily on the ingredients
being super-fresh.

10 EASY TASTY ANTIPASTI

Santini, my family's restaurant, turned 25 last year. I have used a quarter of a century's worth of orders as inspiration for this list of popular quick antipasti, and included dishes that have outsold other, more elaborate, appetizers year after year. This proves that certain culinary bastions are so firmly planted in people's palates that it will take a lot more than a fad to uproot them.

I know that these are not all entirely raw, but forgive me this slight bending of my structure for the book to accommodate these before the main dishes that follow, just as antipasti are meant to be enjoyed. Each antipasti dish serves 4.

1 TRICOLORE WITH ROASTED VINE TOMATOES & AVOCADO

Well ahead, snip the tomato bunches into little sprigs, with 3–4 tomatoes on each sprig. Arrange on a baking tray and lightly dust with confectioners' sugar, drizzle with olive oil, and season with salt and pepper. Place in a preheated low oven (250°F) until the tomatoes begin to soften but are still firm, 7–10 minutes. Let cool.

When ready to serve, arrange a sprig of tomatoes, 3–4 mozzarella balls, and a quarter of an avocado, thinly sliced, in a fan shape on each plate. Drizzle the plate with extra virgin olive oil, season with salt flakes and freshly ground black pepper, and garnish with a fresh basil leaf. Serve with crusty bread and balsamic vinegar.

10 ounces cherry tomatoes on the vine
½ tablespoon confectioners' sugar
extra virgin olive oil
12 bocconcini di buffala (small mozzarella balls), more or less, depending on size
1 ripe avocado, peeled and pitted
salt flakes and freshly ground black pepper
4 sprigs of fresh basil
crusty bread and balsamic vinegar to serve

2 PROSCIUTTO-WRAPPED MOZZARELLA BALLS

Fry the mozzarella wraps in a little oil in a nonstick pan for a few minutes until the prosciutto begins to color and crisp up. Arrange a handful of arugula leaves in the center of each plate and top with 3 wraps per person. Mix the tapenade with a couple of tablespoons of oil and drizzle over each plate. Sprinkle with black pepper and serve immediately.

12 'rolled and wrapped' bocconcini di mozzarella in slices of prosciutto (see pages 144–5)
olive oil
2 ounces fresh arugula leaves
2 tablespoons green or black tapenade
extra virgin olive oil
black pepper

3 ROSE SCALLOPS

Lightly season the scallops with Rose stardust and place 2 in each shell. Sprinkle a pinch each of the crumbs and lime zest on top of each scallop. Grill until the crumbs begin to color and the scallop is firm to the touch. Finish off with a drizzle of olive oil, a squeeze of lime juice, a pinch of parsley, and more Rose stardust. Serve in the shells.

VARIATIONS You can add chopped garlic and parsley to the crumbs for extra flavor. For a more traditional result, the Rose stardust can be replaced with salt and pepper, and the lime with lemon. King prawns, peeled (cooked or raw) and threaded on skewers can replace the scallops in this dish. If using a bamboo skewer, first soak it in water to prevent it charring.

I like to add some gold bling (page 40) to turn this dish into pure magic.
8 large scallops and 4 scallop shells
Rose stardust (page 39)
1 tablespoon fine bread crumbs
grated zest and juice of 1 lime
2 tablespoons extra virgin olive oil
1 teaspoon finely chopped fresh flat-leaf parsley

4 UMAMI PLATE

Arrange on each plate 3 sun-dried tomatoes, a couple of pieces of Parmigiano, a spoonful each of green and black olives, mushrooms, artichokes, and 3 slices of prosciutto, some butter and 2 anchovies drizzled in truffle oil. Do not overfill the plate as it will look messy; cut down quantities to suit the plate/board you are using. Give each person a ramekin with a drizzle of olive oil and a splash of balsamic vinegar, or, better still, one of each. Serve with a basket of bread and breadsticks.

12 sun-dried tomatoes, drained if in oil
12 small rough bite-sized pieces of Parmigiano Reggiano (Parmesan cheese)
4 tablespoons marinated green olives from the deli counter
4 tablespoons marinated black olives from the deli counter
1 jar of preserved mushrooms in oil
1 jar of artichoke pieces in oil
12 slices of prosciutto di Parma
a little butter
8 salted anchovies
truffle oil
extra virgin olive oil
balsamic vinegar
mixed Italian breads and breadsticks

5 WILD MUSHROOM TRIFOLATA

Heat the olive oil in a large frying pan, add the garlic, and let it sizzle until it begins to color. Add the mushrooms and sauté until they soften. Splash with the wine and toss until they begin to caramelize. Season with salt and pepper, and sprinkle with chopped parsley. Toss over a high heat and serve immediately with a drizzle of truffle oil and some arugula leaves and Parmesan shavings over each portion. Serve with toasted paper-thin Sardinian carta di musica or any toasted Italian bread.

VARIATION If you can't run to the truffle oil, add a squeeze of lemon juice and 1 or 2 tablespoons butter with the parsley.

large glug of olive oil
2 garlic cloves, thinly sliced
14 ounces mixed wild mushrooms whole or portobello/shiitake, roughly sliced
splash of white wine
salt flakes and freshly ground black pepper
handful of chopped fresh flat-leaf parsley
handful of fresh arugula leaves, to serve
4 drizzles of truffle oil, to serve
Parmesan shavings, to serve
toasted paper-thin Sardinian carta di musica, or any toasted Italian bread, to serve

6 CRAB SALAD WITH POMEGRANATE & MINT

Mix the crabmeat and herbs, and dress with the olive oil mixed with the juice of one of the lemons, a little salt, and some ground black pepper. Cut the lettuces into quarters and place two on each plate. Divide the crab mixture into 4 and put a pile in the center of each plate, with the lettuce wedges fanning out. Scatter over some pomegranate seeds and decorate with a fresh mint leaf, ground black pepper, and a wedge cut from the other lemon.

10–14 ounces white crabmeat
handful of fresh flat-leaf parsley, chopped
handful of fresh mint leaves, chopped
seeds from 1 pomegranate
glug of olive oil
2 lemons
salt flakes and freshly ground
    black pepper
2 Baby Gem lettuces, cut in wedges

7 POACHED ASPARAGUS WITH ORANGE MAYONNAISE

Mix the mayonnaise with the orange zest and juice, and the Grand Marnier. Set aside (this can be made earlier and stored in the refrigerator). Steam the asparagus until just tender and serve hot or cold, seasoned, drizzled with olive oil, and scattered with almonds. Serve the orange mayonnaise on the side.

½ pound mayonnaise
    (although I use Hellmann's for this)
grated zest and juice of 1 orange
1 tablespoon Grand Marnier or
    other orange liqueur
1⅔ pounds fresh asparagus stalks
salt flakes and freshly ground
    black pepper
extra virgin olive oil
handful of toasted almonds

8 PRAWN STAR

Toss the avocado and arugula in the olive oil and lime juice, and season with Rose stardust. Arrange the arugula and avocado salad in the center of each plate and top with the cooked prawns. Spoon cocktail sauce over the prawns only and decorate with a pinch of Rose stardust and a lime wedge.

VARIATION I like to give this real star quality by adding a sprinkling of gold bling (see page 40).

2 ripe avocados, halved, pitted,
    peeled, and cut in cubes
3 handfuls of fresh wild arugula, roughly
    chopped into fork-sized pieces
3 limes, juice of of 1 and the others halved,
    for garnish
Rose stardust (page 39) or salt flakes
    and freshly ground black pepper
10 ounces peeled cooked king prawns
    or tiger prawns
Pink cocktail sauce (see page 27—you
    can use bought mayonnaise instead
    of making it)

9 CAESAR WEDGE

This dish is a cross between two very popular Italian/American dishes: the iceberg wedge, which is usually served with blue cheese dressing, and the classic favorite Caesar Salad.

First, make the dressing: blend the garlic, mustard, and vinegar with a couple of pinches of salt in a food processor. Add the mayonnaise and anchovies, if using them, and blend. Slowly add the oil in a steady stream until the mixture has a thick dressing consistency. Fold in the Parmesan cheese using a spatula and season with salt, pepper, Worcestershire sauce, and lemon juice.

Remove and discard the outer leaves from the lettuce and cut it into 4 wedges. Place a wedge on each plate and spoon the dressing across the middle of the wedge, leaving the points free. Scatter with chopped chives and ideally serve with crusty garlic bread.

1 tightly packed iceberg lettuce
handful of chives
crusty garlic bread, to serve

FOR THE QUICK CAESAR DRESSING
3 garlic cloves, crushed
1 tablespoon Dijon mustard
1 tablespoon white wine vinegar
salt flakes and freshly ground
  black pepper
2 heaped tablespoons Hellmann's
  mayonnaise
3 anchovy fillets in oil, drained and
  rinsed (optional)
4 tablespoons extra virgin olive oil
1 tablespoon grated Parmesan cheese
dash of Worcestershire sauce
squeeze of lemon juice

10 FIVE-SENSES SALAD

This simple salad is guaranteed to make you come to your senses, providing all five tastes in one delicious mouthful. It also makes a delicious appetizer when served with bresaola, Italian cured beef: top 4 slices of the beef per person with a generous spoonful of the salad.

Remove and discard the outer layers and cores of the fennel and endive. Slice the fennel into ¼-inch discs and the endive into ½-inch pieces. Mix the capers and anchovies in a bowl with the olive oil, garlic, lemon juice, and parsley. Season to taste. Toss the fennel and endive in this dressing and serve with lemon wedges, the raisin sourdough bread, and unsalted butter.

4 fennel bulbs
4 heads of Belgian endive
2 tablespoons capers, rinsed and chopped
5–8 anchovies in oil, drained and chopped
4 tablespoons extra virgin olive oil
1 garlic clove, crushed
juice of 1 lemon
1 tablespoon fresh flat-leaf parsley,
  finely chopped (optional)
salt flakes and freshly ground
  black pepper

TO SERVE
1 lemon, cut in wedges
8 pieces of very thinly sliced sourdough
  raisin bread
four 1-ounce pieces of unsalted butter

BASIC CARPACCIO

Carpaccio is said to have been invented in 1950 by Giuseppe Cipriani, founder of the legendary Harry's Bar in Venice, for the Contessa Amalia Nani Mocenigo, who had been advised by her doctor to eat raw meat. The name for this new dish was inspired by a Vittore Carpaccio exhibition that was showing in Venice at the time, and reflects the vivid flesh-red depicted in his artworks.

1 pound middle-cut beef fillet
3 ounces fresh arugula leaves
2 ounces Parmesan shavings
freshly ground black pepper
1 lemon, quartered

FOR THE CARPACCIO SAUCE
1 cup mayonnaise
2–3 teaspoons Worcestershire sauce
squeeze of fresh lemon juice
1 teaspoon Dijon mustard
splash of brandy
salt flakes and white pepper
3 tablespoons milk

1 Wrap the beef in plastic wrap and put in the freezer for 1 hour to firm up.
2 Meanwhile, make the sauce: mix all ingredients together, adding just enough milk to give the sauce the desired consistency, just coating the back of a spoon.
3 Slice the firmed-up beef into thin rounds about ⅛ inch thick. You can also cut slightly thicker pieces, put them between two sheets of plastic wrap and flatten with a rolling pin.
4 Cover a chilled plate with the beef slices. If not serving immediately (it is much better if you do), cover each plate with plastic wrap and refrigerate to avoid the meat discoloring.
5 To serve, drizzle the meat with the sauce criss-crossing the plate and top with arugula leaves, Parmesan shavings, and a good grinding of black pepper. Serve with lemon wedges.

RICH & THIN

VENISON & MUSHROOM CARPACCIO

1 pound venison fillet
4 portobellini or 8 chestnut mushrooms, thinly sliced
3 ounces pecorino cheese shavings
salt flakes and freshly ground black pepper
drizzle of truffle oil
2 lemons, halved

Chill the venison as above for about 1 hour. Thinly slice and arrange on chilled plates. Scatter with the mushroom slices, followed by the cheese shavings. Season and drizzle with truffle oil. Serve with a lemon half.

SALMON & ROSE CARPACCIO

1 pound organic salmon fillet
1 pink grapefruit, peeled and thinly sliced, removing seeds
couple of sprigs of fresh dill
drizzle of extra virgin olive oil
squeeze of lime juice
splash of grappa or vodka
Rose stardust (page 39)
salt flakes

Chill the salmon as above for about 30 minutes. Thinly slice and arrange on chilled plates. Quarter the grapefruit rounds and scatter over the salmon with dill sprigs. Dress with a drizzle of oil, squeeze of lime juice, and splash of grappa or vodka. Sprinkle with Rose stardust and season with salt.

VARIATION I think this dish looks beautiful dusted with gold or silver flakes (see page 40).

TUNA & ORANGE CARPACCIO

1 pound tuna fillet
2 oranges, peeled and thinly sliced
1 small red onion, very thinly sliced
1 large fennel bulb, very thinly sliced
drizzle of olive oil
splash of Worcestershire sauce
Renaissance stardust (page 39)
freshly ground black pepper

Chill the tuna as above for about 40 minutes. Thinly slice and arrange on chilled plates. Arrange the orange slices over the tuna. Top with the very thinly sliced red onion and fennel. Drizzle with olive oil and a few drops of Worcestershire sauce. Season with Renaissance stardust and black pepper.

SEA BASS & SESAME CARPACCIO

1 pound sea bass fillets
1 tablespoon Furikake (see page 39)

FOR THE DRESSING
3 tablespoons olive oil
1 tablespoon lemon or yuzu juice
½ teaspoon freshly grated gingerroot
splash of soy sauce

Chill the fish for 30 minutes as above. Thinly slice and arrange on chilled plates. Mix the dressing ingredients together and drizzle over the bass. Sprinkle with Furikake. Serve immediately.

VARIATION The sea bass can be replaced by 12 scallops, any roe removed. Chill for 10 minutes only until firm. Thinly slice as above. Again, I like to bling this up with gold (see page 40).

BASIC CEVICHE

Originally South American, ceviche is now very popular all over the world. In this refreshing and light dish, raw fish is 'cooked' using the acidic juice of citrus fruits rather than heat. The produce and flavors of Italy lend themselves exceptionally well to this idea. Experiment with flavors, but remember to keep the acidity levels high; otherwise there will be no 'cooking' and your ceviche will be slimy. Don't be tempted to prepare ceviche too far ahead, as the acid continues to break down the protein and the fish will lose its texture.

1 pound skinned boneless fresh fish (sea bass, cod, salmon, tuna, sole, scallops, or any lean white fish), cut in cubes
juice of 3 lemons
juice of 3 limes
juice of 1 orange
1 garlic clove, crushed
1 fresh red chili pepper, seeded and finely chopped
handful of fresh cilantro, chopped
handful of fresh flat-leaf parsley, finely chopped
salt flakes and freshly ground black pepper
1 red onion, thinly sliced

TO SERVE
1 Baby Gem lettuce
Rose stardust (page 39, optional)

1 Combine all the ingredients except the onion and mix well.
2 Place the onion slices on the top of the mixture, cover, and refrigerate for at least 2–3 hours.
3 Serve chilled in the Baby Gem leaves. Sprinkle with Rose stardust for extra flavor.

CEVICHE & TARTARE

BASIC STEAK TARTARE

Steak tartare became fashionable in the 1950s and was known in smart Parisian restaurants as steak *américaine*, a sort of hamburger that skipped the griddle and cut straight to the chase.

SERVES 4
1 pound fillet of beef, minced
1½ tablespoons chopped gherkins
3 tablespoons finely chopped fresh flat-leaf parsley
1½ tablespoons chopped capers
1½ tablespoons finely chopped shallot
3 tablespoons tomato ketchup
3 teaspoons Worcestershire sauce
1 tablespoon Dijon mustard
generous splash of Tabasco sauce
1 tablespoon olive oil
salt flakes and freshly ground black pepper
4 egg yolks

VARIATION This can be transformed into a burger by adding 2–3 handfuls of fine bread crumbs (see page 47).

1 Combine all the ingredients except the egg yolks.
2 Divide the mixture between 4 chilled plates and make a well in the middle of each for a whole egg yolk.
3 Put the egg yolks in the wells.
4 Lightly drizzle the plate with olive oil, salt flakes, and freshly ground black pepper. Serve immediately.

BASIC RICOTTA DIP

Serendipity is the effect by which you can accidentally discover something useful, especially while looking for something else entirely.

I have often reached culinary ecstasy by dervish-ly whirling random and unsuspecting ingredients in my blender. Avocados, cooked canned legumes, soft cheeses, and curds make the perfect fellow conspirators for the madness in this method.

½ pound ricotta cheese
handful of chopped fresh mixed
    herbs (basil, mint, chervil,
    marjoram, parsley)
½ teaspoon chili flakes
    (optional)
grated zest of 1 lemon
salt flakes and freshly ground
    black pepper
1 tablespoon tapenade (green or
    black)
extra virgin olive oil
splash of vinegar

1 Turn the ricotta out on a serving dish. Slightly squash and spread it with the back of a fork.
2 Sprinkle with chopped herbs, chili flakes, lemon zest, salt, and black pepper, and drizzle with the tapenade mixed with some olive oil and a splash of vinegar, plus some more extra virgin olive oil.

VARIATION The tapenade can be replaced with pesto in this recipe, or omitted altogether.

SEREN-DIP-ITY

WHITE BEAN & POMEGRANATE DIP

14-ounce can of cannellini
    beans, drained and rinsed
2 tablespoons white balsamic
    vinegar
salt flakes and freshly ground
    black pepper
3 ounces feta cheese, crumbled
2½ ounces pomegranate seeds
chopped mint
Rose stardust (optional,
    page 39)
¾ cup extra virgin olive oil
lemon juice

In a food processor, blend the beans with the vinegar and seasoning to taste. Put in a shallow bowl and top with feta, pomegranate seeds, mint to taste, and Rose stardust, if using it. Drizzle with olive oil and lemon juice to taste.

VARIATION I add a sprinkle of gold flakes (page 40) to give a new dimension to this dip.

EGGPLANT & LAVENDER DIP

3 eggplants
1 garlic clove
6 tablespoons olive oil
juice of 1 lemon
½ teaspoon Lavender stardust
    (page 39)
1 tablespoon toasted cumin
    seeds
1 teaspoon lavender seeds

Put the eggplants on a baking tray and bake in an oven preheated to 350°F until shrivelled on the outside and soft and mushy inside, about 30 minutes. Remove the skin and blend the flesh in a food processor with the garlic, olive oil, lemon juice, and stardust to a smooth paste. Serve in a decorative bowl, sprinkled with toasted cumin and lavender seeds.

VARIATION I sprinkle silver flakes (page 40) on mine.

TASTY TOMATO DIP

10 ounces cherry tomatoes
1 garlic clove
1 heaped tablespoon capers
1 heaped tablespoon pitted
    black olives in oil, drained
2 anchovies in oil, drained
    (optional)
handful of fresh basil leaves
3 tablespoons olive oil
juice of ½ lemon
salt flakes and freshly ground
    black pepper

Pulse all the ingredients in a food processor until they form an easily spooned dip, but do not over-process and try to retain some of the texture of the ingredients. Season to taste.

GORGONZOLA & MASCARPONE DIP

5 ounces Gorgonzola Piccante
½ pound mascarpone cheese
2 ounces dried prunes,
    coarsely chopped
2 ounces toasted flaked almonds
drizzle of balsamic vinegar
drizzle of extra virgin olive oil
freshly ground black pepper
snipped fresh chives

Beat the Gorgonzola in a bowl with a wooden spoon until smooth, then fold in the mascarpone without combining totally. Carefully fold in the chopped prunes and transfer to a serving bowl. Finish by scattering with toasted almonds and a drizzle each of balsamic vinegar and olive oil, some black pepper, and chives.

WATER

'I was cooked'

I. BOILING (PAGES 68–77)

The recipes in this section are all about the 'bubble' without the 'toil and trouble'.

II. ABSORPTION & REDUCTION (PAGES 78–107)

The recipes in this section are all about encouraging ingredients like rice to absorb water and flavors.

III. POACHING (PAGES 108–111)

The recipes in this section are all about the art of cooking very gently in barely simmering water.

IV. BAGNO-MARIA (PAGES 112–115)

The recipes in this section are all about cooking even more gently in water that is merely hot.

INNOCENT (SWEET POTATO) SOUP

This recipe—named 'Innocent' soup by a deep thinker who remarked on the soup's earnest qualities—can be applied to almost any vegetable and can be additionally seasoned with appropriate herbs. For vegetables that do not naturally 'mush up', add one large potato for a smooth finish. Use ground white pepper for pale-colored soups.

Heat the oil in a large saucepan. Add the onion and garlic, and cook over a moderate heat until softened and glassy but not browned. Add the sweet potatoes and herbs, and toss with the onion, garlic, and oil. Cover with cold water, add the stock cube and some pepper, and boil until all ingredients are soft and ready to blend. Remove from the heat and process with a hand blender until smooth. Adjust the seasoning.

TASTY TRANSFORMATIONS

SUGGESTED TOPPING

CHILI SHRIMP RELISH (PAGE 31)
OR LEMON MASCARPONE & SCORCHED ALMONDS (PAGE 70)

SUGGESTED FLAVOR BOMB

TOMATO, PEPPER, ORANGE, AND CINNAMON PASTE (PAGE 43)

SERVES 4–6
2 tablespoons olive oil
1 onion, quartered
2 garlic cloves
4½ pounds sweet potatoes, peeled
  and roughly chopped
leaves from a sprig of fresh thyme
1 vegetable stock cube
salt flakes and freshly ground
  white pepper

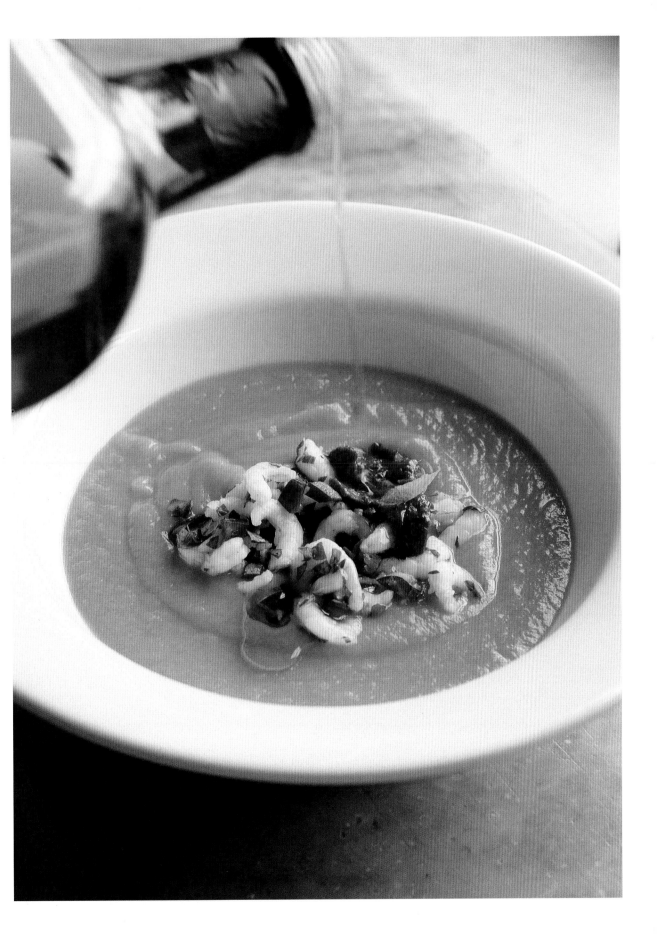

NONNA MAGGIE'S QUICK CURRIED LENTIL SOUP

Not strictly Italian, but then again, who cares? There are Indians in Italy and Italians in India . . . all eating lentils.

Heat the oil in a large saucepan, add the onion and garlic, and sweat until translucent, taking care not to let them color. Add the curry paste and fry briefly, then add the bay leaves and lentils, and cook, stirring, with the curry mixture for several minutes so they absorb the flavor. Add 6 cups of cold water and the crumbled stock cubes. Bring to a boil, then reduce the heat, and simmer until the soup has a creamy consistency. If the soup gets too thick during cooking, add a little more water. Adjust the seasoning and serve topped with a drizzle of extra virgin olive oil and a pinch of cumin seeds.

VARIATION For a more authentically Italian version, omit the curry and add some chopped tomatoes and chopped fresh herbs about 10 minutes before the end of cooking.

TASTY TRANSFORMATIONS

SUGGESTED TOPPING Lemon Mascarpone & Scorched Almonds
Mix 4 ounces mascarpone with a teaspoon of the juice and all the grated zest from 1 lemon, and season with salt and black pepper and salt to taste. Toast 3 handfuls of nibbed or flaked almonds in a dry nonstick frying pan over a gentle heat for about 5 minutes until just colored. Remove them from the pan just before they reach the color you want. Top the soup with a dollop of the lemon cream, and sprinkle with the scorched almonds.

SUGGESTED FLAVOR BOMB
GARLIC, SWEET BASIL, AND ALMOND PASTE (PAGE 43)

SERVES 4–6
4 tablespoons olive oil
1 large Spanish onion, finely chopped
3 garlic cloves, peeled and cut in half
2 teaspoons curry paste (or to taste)
2 bay leaves
2 cups red lentils, well washed and checked for stones
2 vegetable stock cubes
salt flakes and freshly ground black pepper
drizzle of extra virgin olive oil, to serve
sprinkling of cumin seeds, to serve

MINESTRONE

The vegetables added at the end can vary according to the season; in spring, for example, try adding chopped asparagus and fresh fava beans.

Drain the beans and rinse well under cold water. Heat the olive oil in a large pan and add the onions, garlic, and pancetta, if using it. Cook over a moderate heat until the onions are soft and the pancetta is crisping up but not browning. Add the tomatoes with 11 cups of water, the stock cubes, beans, marjoram, sage, and tomato paste. Skim off any froth that rises to the surface. Reduce the heat, cover, and simmer until the beans are tender, about 1½–2 hours. Add the celery and carrots, and cook for 10 minutes, then add the remaining vegetables. Cook until these are tender. Adjust the seasoning and add the chopped parsley and basil just before serving.

VARIATIONS If you like, a couple of handfuls of small pasta shapes can be added towards the end of cooking. Use the cooking times on the pack as a guide to when to add the pasta. It is important to know that once pasta has gone in you really need to eat it all, as when it is left over it swells and becomes slimy. I take out the portions I need for that meal from the big pot and add the pasta then to avoid the problem.

TASTY TRANSFORMATIONS

SUGGESTED TOPPING
A DRIZZLE OF EXTRA VIRGIN OLIVE OIL AND GRATED PARMESAN CHEESE

SUGGESTED FLAVOR BOMB
A DOLLOP OF BASIL PESTO (PAGE 29)

SERVES 4–6

5 ounces navy beans, soaked overnight in water
3 tablespoons olive oil
2 onions, finely chopped
2 garlic cloves
2½ ounces pancetta, diced or finely chopped (optional)
5 tomatoes, chopped
2 vegetable stock cubes
1 tablespoon chopped fresh marjoram
3 fresh sage leaves
2 tablespoons tomato paste
2 celery ribs, finely chopped
2 carrots, diced
½ savoy cabbage, finely shredded
2 zucchini, diced
2 handfuls of fresh/frozen peas (optional)
salt flakes and freshly ground black pepper
handful of fresh flat-leaf parsley, finely chopped
handful of fresh basil, finely chopped

PASTA E FAGIOLI

Like many Italian dishes, this soup is based on a soffritto. *Soffrigere* is to fry lightly in Italian, and a *soffritto* is therefore a 'lightly fried' chopped mixture of carrot, onion, and celery, often with added herbs.

First make the soffritto base: in a food processor, pulse the onion, garlic, carrot, and celery into fine pieces. Heat the oil in a large heavy-based pan and fry the vegetables with the parsley until the onions become glassy but not colored.

Drain the beans and add them to the soffritto with the bay leaf and rosemary. Fry together for a moment, stirring well. Put in a large pan and add water to cover by 2 inches. Add half the chopped tomatoes and the bacon, if using it, and cook gently for 3–4 hours until the beans are soft, stirring occasionally to prevent sticking and adding more boiling water if needed.

When the beans are cooked, remove a third and set aside. Remove the bacon and discard. Using a mouli sieve or hand blender (the former will give a better result), blend the remaining mixture in the pot until smooth.

Return the whole beans to the pot. Adjust the seasoning and bring back to a boil. Add the pasta and cook until it is al dente. Turn off the heat and allow the soup to stand for 10 minutes.

Serve each bowlful with a drizzle of extra virgin olive oil, a sprinkling of chopped celery leaves, a spoonful of the remaining chopped tomato, and some grated Parmesan.

TASTY TRANSFORMATIONS

SUGGESTED FLAVOR BOMB
BLACK OLIVE, CAPER, & WALNUT PASTE (PAGE 43)

SERVES 4–6
1 pound dried borlotti beans, soaked
  overnight in cold water
1 bay leaf
sprig of fresh rosemary
6 tomatoes, seeded and chopped
6–8 slices of streaky bacon (optional)
salt flakes and freshly ground
  black pepper
7 ounces short tubular pasta or 5 ounces
  cut fresh pasta for a more delicate finish
extra virgin olive oil, to serve
grated Parmesan cheese, to serve

FOR THE SOFFRITTO
2 onions, quartered
2 garlic cloves
1 carrot, coarsely chopped
1 celery rib, coarsely chopped, plus
  a handful of chopped celery leaves,
  to serve
3 tablespoons olive oil
generous handful of fresh flat-leaf
  parsley, chopped

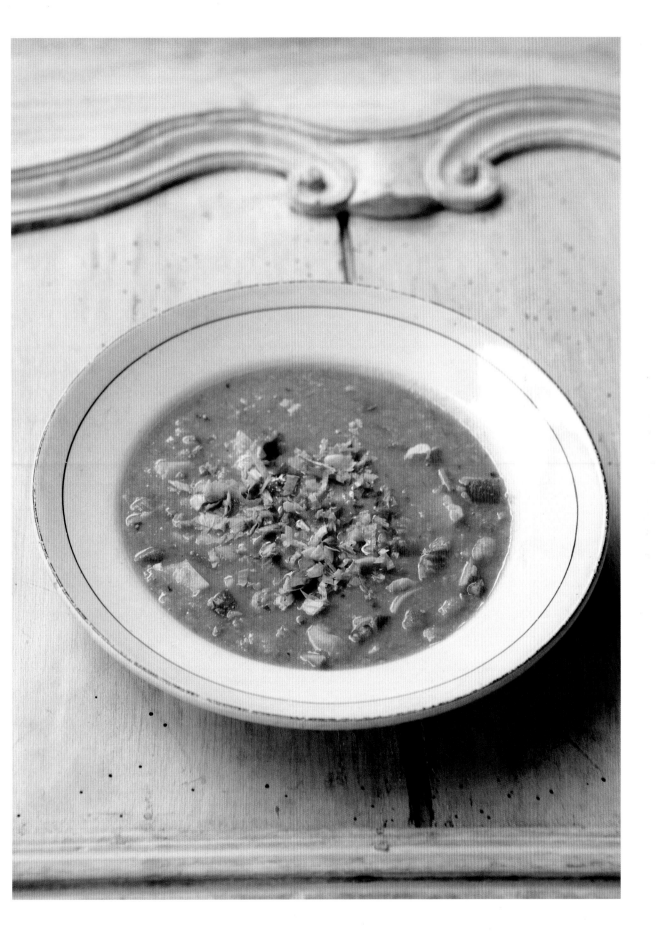

GARIBALDI'S FISH SOUP

Named after the Italian revolutionary Garibaldi, who was born in Nice and therefore vehemently opposed his city being returned to the French by the Italian royals, the Savoia (Savoy), in 1860. This fish soup straddles the Italo-French borders and represents all that is delicious within that region, regardless of politics and boundaries.

Heat the oil in a large heavy-based saucepan. Add the onion, garlic, and chili, and fry until the onion begins to soften and become glassy. Add the anchovies, potato cubes, parsley, orange zest and juice, saffron, and bay leaf, and stir well. Splash with the vermouth or wine and cook over a high heat for a minute to allow the alcohol to evaporate. Add the fish stock and tomato sugo, lower the heat, and cook slowly for 20 minutes, until the potato is soft but not disintegrating.

Just before serving, add the shellfish and fish gently, and simmer until the mussels open and the monkfish is cooked. Add another drop of vermouth or wine for extra flavor, adjust the seasoning, and serve drizzled with a little chili oil or the Red pepper and orange oil.

TASTY TRANSFORMATIONS

SUGGESTED TOPPING
Ciabatta Croutons with Spicy Orange Mayonnaise & Gruyère Cheese
Add a few drops of Orange mayonnaise (page 27). Toast a slice of ciabatta bread, spread with the spicy mayonnaise and top with grated Gruyère cheese. If using a large oven-ready bowl to serve, cover the soup with these croutons and place under the broiler until the cheese begins to bubble. Sprinkle with Gremolata (page 158).

SUGGESTED FLAVOR BOMB
TOMATO, PEPPER, ORANGE, AND CINNAMON PASTE (PAGE 43)

SERVES 4–6

4 tablespoons olive oil
1 large onion, thinly sliced
2 garlic cloves, thinly sliced
1 large red chili, seeded if you prefer and thinly sliced
5 anchovies in oil, drained
1 large potato, cubed (fingernail-sized)
1 large handful of chopped fresh flat-leaf parsley, plus more to serve
grated zest and juice of 1 orange
1 pinch of saffron threads
1 bay leaf
⅔ cup vermouth (Martini Bianco) or white wine, plus more to finish
6 cups good fish stock
10 ounces tomato sugo (page 84) or good commercial marinara sauce without seafood, sieved
14 ounces mussels (discard open ones that don't close on being tapped), beards removed
4 ounces raw tiger prawns (shell on)
7 ounces baby squid, cut in rings
10 ounces monkfish, any membrane removed and the fish cut in large chunks
3 ½ ounces bay scallops
drizzle of chili oil or Red pepper and orange oil (page 45), to serve

COMPLETE MEAL CHICKEN SOUP

Your words are my food,
your breath my wine.
You are everything to me.

SARAH BERNHARDT

This is a family favorite and feeds four for a couple of days, so it is ideal if you have a busy week—a one-stop feel-good nutritious meal. Both the common cold and the more serious 'Man Flu' can be cured with this ancient potion. For medicinal purposes, up the garlic to at least 5 or 6 cloves.

Rinse the chicken and giblets in cold water and put in a tall pan with the other ingredients. Fill with cold water until the chicken is completely covered, about 12 cups. Bring to a boil, lower the heat, and simmer gently for about 1 hour, 20 minutes, or until the liquid is a flavorsome stock and the chicken is falling apart. Adjust the seasoning and drain the liquid into a separate pan. Remove chicken and giblets, and set aside to cool. Discard the vegetables and herbs.

Pick the meat from the cooled chicken and set aside. To feed 4–5, drain off half the soup. This can be stored in the refrigerator or freezer when cool. I keep mine in the refrigerator and use it for supper later in the week. Bring the rest to a boil and add 1–2 handfuls of pasta or rice per person and one for the pot. Follow pasta cooking times and, about 3 minutes before the pasta is due to be ready, add the kale and a handful of picked chicken meat per person.

I chop the giblets and add to my bowl, but other family members are not so keen. Therefore check out your audience before adding these contentious nuggets to the general pot. Serve in large bowls with grated Parmesan cheese.

VARIATION The other half of this soup can also be transformed into chicken risotto as on page 103, replacing that stock with the chicken broth and adding the chicken pieces and kale, etc. in the last 10 minutes to cook.

TASTY TRANSFORMATIONS

SUGGESTED TOPPING
Mixed Sesame & Seaweed Stardust
Add a tablespoon of grated hard cheese (I like mature Cheddar) in the center of each bowl, drizzle with extra virgin olive oil and sprinkle with Furikake stardust (page 39). For a magical dish that is way more than the sum of its parts, I like to finish off with a tiny sprinkling of gold dust (page 40).

SUGGESTED FLAVOR BOMB
PARMESAN & PROSCIUTTO PASTE (PAGE 43)

MAKES ENOUGH FOR 8
1 whole large chicken,
*   preferably organic, with giblets*
2 Spanish onions, quartered
2 celery ribs, each snapped in two
2 small or 1 large carrot(s), cut in two
2 leeks, cut in two and well rinsed
2 sprigs of fresh flat-leaf parsley
2 sprigs of fresh thyme
1 large bay leaf
3 garlic cloves
12 black peppercorns (a palmful)
1 tablespoon rock salt

TO SERVE (PER 4 PEOPLE)
5–10 handfuls of small pasta shapes
*   (pastina) or arborio rice*
4 handfuls of shredded kale,
*   cavolo nero or savoy cabbage*
freshly grated Parmesan cheese

THE ARCHITECTURE OF PASTA

The architecture of pasta is an art and not remotely random. Each and every pasta shape that you see or taste has been carefully and precisely designed to catch, trap, or repel its saucy counterparts. One brand leader even went as far as asking world-renowned car designer Giorgetto Giugiaro to develop the Maserati Quattroporte of pasta shapes, and, although not ultimately such a successful project as a notion, it clearly illustrates how seriously Italians take their pasta!

There are hundreds of different pasta shapes and they fall into two basic categories, fresh and dry. In Italy, dry pasta (*pasta secca*) is made from durum wheat or semolina flour, cooks to a perfect al dente consistency, and uncooked it can last virtually forever. Fresh pasta (*pasta fresca*) contains eggs and is softer than dried pasta; consequently, the cooking times are far shorter and it has a shorter shelf-life, as it has to be stored chilled. The concept of al dente is quite different in this category, as you will never get that 'bite' with it, so just strive to keep the texture firm and take care not to overcook, as it will then literally fall apart. There is also dried 'fresh' pasta and this falls somewhere in between the two. Fettuccine and tagliatelle in this category are brilliant, and I personally prefer them as they do come closer to al dente than fresh pasta.

With regards to making my own pasta, I would sooner milk my own cow! Don't get me wrong; I have made miles of the stuff (but have been paid to do so). I would only do this as a fun afternoon with the children. It would also be fair to say that, apart from being a bit of a waste of time, it is not as easy as it looks, or rather more difficult than the very simple mixing of flour, eggs, water, a pinch of salt, and, in some cases, a drop of olive oil. Colorings or flavorings, such as spinach, squid ink, saffron, herbs, chili, tomato or beet, are often added to the original *impasto*, in which case the egg quantity may need to be adjusted to accommodate these introductions.

It is the *stendere*, or rolling out, that is the real bind and requires a feel in the fingertips. Pasta must be rolled out until almost translucent, depending on the use, but overworking will cause the surface to get too smooth and become rubbery. With small amounts of dough I prefer to mix and roll by hand with a wooden rolling pin; at work I use an industrial mixer and an electric Imperia pasta machine.

BASIC PASTA ALL'UOVO (FRESH EGG PASTA)

This recipe was given to me by a wonderful couple whose magical restaurant, Trattoria La Rosa in Sant'Agostino, near Ferrara, is famed for its pasta. Emilia-Romagna is the region best known for fresh pasta, so this is definitely from the horse's mouth! If you ever happen to be in the area, drop in and tell Francesco and Adriana that you are a friend of mine! It is really important to find proper pasta-making flour, which is very finely milled. Such flour always has the words 'type 00' or 'farina tipo 00' (*doppio zero*) on the packaging. Adriana doesn't add salt to her pasta, but I can't resist a pinch. In some parts of Italy a tablespoon of olive oil is also added for extra elasticity and flavor. It is also really worth investing in good-quality free-range eggs, as it is the yolk that colors the pasta.

SERVES 4–6 (DEPENDING ON WHETHER APPETIZER OR MAIN COURSE)
1 pound type 00 flour
5 whole eggs (the rule is 1 whole egg for every 3 ½ ounces of flour)
pinch of salt

Sieve the flour into a mound on a marble board or clean work surface. Make a well in the center and crack the eggs in one by one; add your pinch of salt, if using it. Some like to use a fork to lightly beat the eggs in the center, drawing in the flour a little at a time, but I prefer to use my fingertips to get a real feel for the dough right from the start. Knead together into a large ball of dough, more like pastry than bread. Leave to rest for 15 minutes to half an hour. Trust me, *you* will need to rest before you start rolling! If working by hand, lightly flour your rolling pin and commence the roll; if using a pasta machine just think how lucky you are! I would recommend working a half or a quarter of your dough at a time so as not to have yards and yards of fragile pasta to deal with. Roll until very thin and almost translucent, then cut in the required shape.

NOTE Since eggs are not manufactured to a standard specification, your dough may be too wet or too dry. If too wet, add a little more flour; if too dry, add a drop of water.

Oh, the comfort, the inexpressible comfort of feeling safe with a person.

GEORGE ELIOT

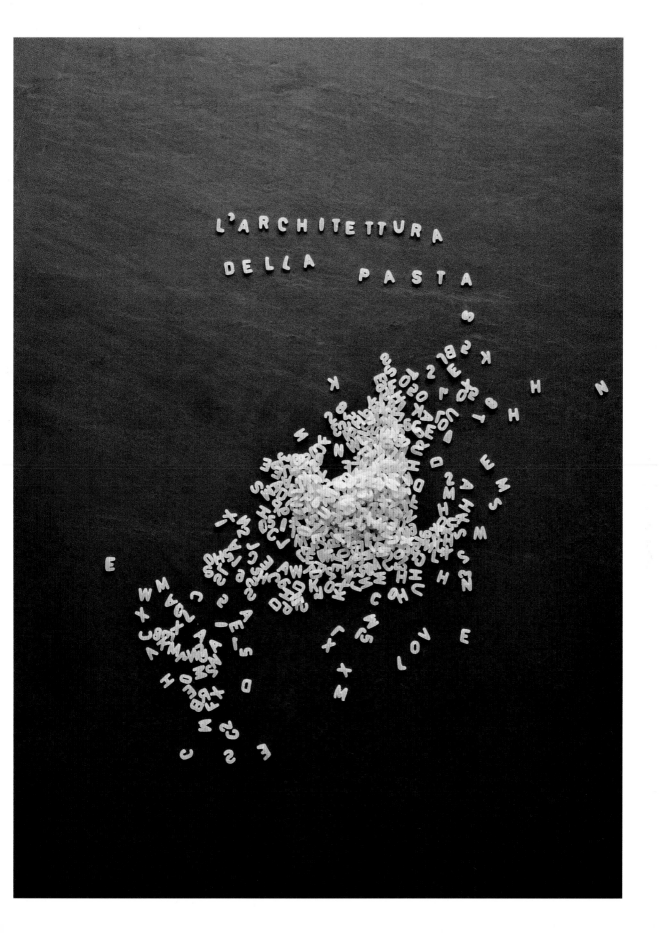

HOW TO COOK PASTA

TOOLS

If you are going to buy just one thing from the equipment list on page 16, I would strongly recommend a proper pasta cooking pot. I first discovered these when I moved to Milan. To my surprise, everyone I met there had one–but nobody had a simple kettle, and water for tea was boiled in a milk pan!

A good pasta pot should have a 5-quart capacity and a large built-in colander. I've had mine for years and use it for everything from soup and stocks to vegetables. It provides a safe and easy way to drain pasta without rushing to the sink: you simply pull the built-in colander up and out, and the water stays in the pot.

Be sure to look for a pot with a minimum capacity of 4 quarts and a large and spacious colander; otherwise, no matter the size of the pot, your pasta will be confined anyway, which defeats the object. The Ferrari of these pots is the Alessi Pasta Set, complete with a steam-releasing lid. This is not cheap and not as big as the one I have at home, but when something looks this good, size does not really matter! If you are not feeling so romantic, a large ordinary saucepan with a 4–5 quart capacity and a large colander in the sink will suffice.

PROCEDURE

1 Fill a large pot with water, cover, and bring to a boil.
NOTE The rule is 4½ cups of water for every 3½ ounces of pasta.
2 When at a good rolling boil, add 1 tablespoon of rock salt (a palm-full) and wait for the water to come back up to a boil.
NOTE The rule is about ¼ ounce of rock salt per 4½ cups of water. When planning to serve your pasta with particularly salty sauces like anchovy, adjust this so as not to over-season.
3 Taste the water for saltiness. You want to make sure that it is salty enough to season your pasta and not too salty to spoil it.
NOTE There's nothing worse than unseasoned pasta. You can work hard making a tasty sauce, but if the pasta you add it to is bland, and/or overcooked, results will be disappointing.
4 Add the pasta to the boiling water and stir. Bring back to a boil and lower the heat slightly to avoid it boiling over. Cook as directed on the packet. Don't cover, as this will cause the pasta to stew (unless you're fortunate enough to have the Alessi pot with the steam-releasing lid).
NOTE Stirring is important, especially with long pastas, to make sure that each strand is released and not stuck in the bottom of the pot like a witch's broom! Once the pasta is free and swimming, there is no need to add oil to stop it from sticking (a bit of a myth), as the rolling water will see to that. Oil is sometimes used in commercial kitchens to prevent large quantities of drained par-cooked pasta sticking.

5 Test the pasta and drain when al dente. As I am sure you already know, Italians eat their pasta *al dente*, which literally means 'to the tooth' or loosely translated as 'with a bite'. Note the cooking time on the packet but test the pasta throughout.

IMPORTANT Remember to drain pasta just before your preferred al dente, because the pasta continues to cook even after draining. So the simile I use, based on the London tube, is–if you want to get out at Baker Street, get the pasta out at Marylebone (one stop before), otherwise you will end up in Regent's Park (a stop too far)! In other words, pasta transforms in a bad way once cooked. Even if you drain and dress on time, leaving the pasta to stew in its own juice at the table will also take you a few stops further than you want to be.

Once dressed, pasta becomes a matter of great urgency and it's very important to tuck in the moment it is cooked. Everything else can wait once the magic words, *a tavola!* are uttered.

WATER–BOIL–SALT–PASTA–STIR–TASTE–DRAIN–DRESS–SERVE

HOW MUCH PASTA?

I haven't specified pasta quantities in the sauce section. This is it.

PASTA ASCIUTTA–DRY PASTA

3½ ounces per person for a one-course meal
2–3 ounces per person for an appetizer
2 ounces per person for pasta added to soups

PASTA FRESCA–FRESH PASTA

3 ounces for a one-course meal
1–1½ ounce(s) per person added to soups

How to mix and match your sauces with your pastas is more difficult. There are no spoken 'set' rules, but there are silent ones. Obviously it is fun to experiment, but there are certain things that to me would just be wrong, Fusilli alla carbonara would be one of them. This is my personal opinion. See my recommendations for pasta shapes to go with the sauces in The Top 10 Classic Pasta Sauces of All Time (page 88). This is me, though, and you may want to break with tradition.

It's a bit like the Parmesan cheese thing; when is it wrong to add it? Tradition says it should not be added to fish or shellfish pastas and risottos, although in some coastal regions of Italy it is perfectly acceptable. I once heard an Italian man ask a waiter to add cheese to his seafood risotto. When the waiter looked horrified he simply retorted:

Saro ignorante, ma mi piace cosi! (Ignorant perhaps, but this is how I like it!)

TOMATO SAUCES EXPOSED

Who was better looking, Elvis or Clark Gable?
Rita Hayworth or Marilyn?

Like a lot of tasty things, each and every one was different but delicious none the less, and it is the same in the world of tomato sauce. Those who know no better talk of fresh tomato sauce as if it is 'the one' and look on *sugo* made with canned tomatoes as an inferior sauce. This is just not so and has never been the case in Italy. Before the days of supermarkets and perennially 'ripe' produce, fresh tomatoes were used when in season for lighter dishes in the sunnier months. These ripe fresh tomatoes were then canned or bottled, and squirreled away for use in the winter as a base for heavier sauces on less sunny days.

We now know that ripe fresh tomatoes are high in glutamates and therefore bursting with umami. Some of this flavor is lost in the preserving process, therefore Italian housewives instinctively added a glutamate-boosting soffritto base to their stored summer treasure. That is it in a nutshell.

In this section you will see how to prepare and love both types of sauce–and others to boot, like the uncooked fresh tomato sauce known as *crudaiola*. There will always be a favorite, but frankly I don't give a damn! While we are on the subject of taste, I taste everything I cook over and over, until I get it just right for me. Remember that things taste different when hot, and also it is important not to over-season in the early part of cooking because, as liquids reduce and flavors mingle, things can change dramatically, as can looks!

Since we are rarely lucky enough to find sweet sun-ripened tomatoes in the supermarkets, it is important to taste the sauce for acidity when seasoning. Fresh tomatoes are usually very acidic, so I add half a teaspoon of superfine sugar. This does not sweeten the sauce but, together with the salt and pepper, merely removes unwanted acidity and balances the flavors. Taste until you get the balance right.

All the pasta sauces in this section serve 4–6, depending on whether the dish is a first or main course.

YOU SAY FRESH TOMATO, I SAY PASSATO!

BASIC **SOFFRITTO**-BASED TOMATO SAUCE (SUGO DI POMODORO)

Soffrigere is to fry lightly, and soffritto is a 'lightly fried' chopped mixture of carrot, onion, and celery, the Three Musketeers of Italian cookery. This swashbuckling trio are chopped in different ways, depending on the recipe.

It's a formula you must remember and the square root of many classic Italian dishes:
Soffritto = onion + celery + carrot + garlic
Apply this formula to the 1+1 = 8 formula on page 20 and you have U-mamma!

This complete and flavorsome sauce freezes brilliantly and is really worth making in bulk and having frozen portions to hand. Passata can be used instead of canned or bottled tomatoes, in which case substitute two 2-pound bottles or 2 pounds whole plum tomatoes squashed between your fingers as they go in.

three 14-ounce cans of chopped tomatoes (plain, not with herbs or anything else 'added value')
large handful of fresh basil leaves
salt flakes and freshly ground black pepper
1 teaspoon sugar

FOR THE SOFFRITTO
1 large Spanish onion, quartered
2 carrots, quartered
2 celery ribs, quartered
3 garlic cloves
olive oil for frying

1 First make the soffritto: pulse the onion, carrots, celery, and garlic in a food processor until everything is chopped to the size of small red lentils.
2 Heat ¼ inch of oil in a large pan, add the soffritto base, and sauté in the oil until the onion becomes translucent–do not allow the mixture to color.
3 Add the tomatoes (I always fill a third of the empty can with water to wash out any lingering pieces and add some extra liquid), torn basil leaves, salt, pepper, and sugar.
4 Cook over a low slow heat, stirring frequently to avoid sticking, for 20–30 minutes, or until the tomato sauce and the oil separate on the surface. Once ready, you should have a rich, tangy tomato sauce.
5 Finally, pass through a fine sieve to remove any pips and bits.

TOMATO & MASCARPONE SAUCE
Heat the required serving of finished base sugo as above and spoon in mascarpone cheese until a creamy pale-pinky sauce is obtained. Adjust the seasoning and heat through but do not boil.

CHILI & CINNAMON SAUCE
Add to the basic soffritto some dried chili flakes and a stick of cinnamon, and proceed as above. A good-quality bottled tomato pasta sauce can be used instead of the basic sauce.

SALAMI & ROSEMARY SAUCE
Add some of the finished basic sauce to 3 ounces of diced salami that has been sautéed in a little oil with a sprig of rosemary. Again, a good-quality bottled tomato pasta sauce can be used instead of the basic sauce.

BASIC FRESH TOMATO SAUCE (POMODORO FRESCO)

This dish requires premium-quality ingredients because there are so few of them in the first place. Use all the tomato and only cut out the woody core; do not remove the skin and seeds. To discard the *corazon* (heart) of a tomato is to let go of much of its umami.

extra virgin olive oil
3 garlic cloves, thinly sliced
2 pounds cherry tomatoes, halved lengthways
large handful of fresh basil leaves, roughly torn
1 teaspoon sugar
salt flakes and freshly ground black pepper

1 Heat ½ inch of oil in a large nonstick frying pan. Toss in the garlic and cook, stirring, for a few minutes to flavor the oil.
2 Just before the garlic begins to color, add the tomatoes, basil, sugar, and salt and pepper to taste.
3 Cook over a low heat for 8–10 minutes, until the tomatoes have broken down but not totally lost their shape.

FRESH TOMATO & BASIL SAUCE WITH RICOTTA & BLACK OLIVE TAPENADE

AS ABOVE, PLUS
1 or 2 tablespoons butter
5 ounces ricotta cheese, crumbled
1 tablespoon black olive tapenade
more fresh basil leaves

Place the butter in the serving bowl, add the drained cooked pasta, and toss with three-quarters of the basic sauce. Top with the remaining sauce and some crumbled ricotta. Drizzle with tapenade and scatter over some more basil leaves.

ALMOND & CHILI SAUCE

Add to the basic sauce 2–3 handfuls of roughly chopped skinned almonds and some chili flakes that have been toasted with the garlic for the basic recipe.

ARUGULA & SHRIMP ARRABIATA SAUCE

Add some cooked peeled shrimp and sizzle before adding the tomatoes. Finish off with torn arugula leaves.

SICILIAN SAUCE

Be daring and add 3-4 drained anchovies in oil, a handful of raisins, and another of pine nuts for a typically Sicilian flavor mix.

AMATRICIANA SAUCE

Sizzle 3 ounces of chopped pancetta and 1 small onion, thinly sliced, in a couple of tablespoons of olive oil with ½ teaspoon of chopped chili. Serve with grated pecorino rather than Parmesan.

ARRABIATA SAUCE

Simply add some fresh or dried chili.

BASIC RAW FRESH TOMATO SAUCE (CRUDO OR CRUDAIOLA)

This is the base for a tepid summer pasta. The heat of the just-drained pasta brings out the aromas and flavors of these simple base ingredients.

2 pounds cherry tomatoes
   (or any sweet juicy tomatoes)
1 garlic clove, squashed
   but whole
1 large handful of basil leaves
extra virgin olive oil
salt flakes and freshly ground
   black pepper

1 Chop the tomatoes into fingernail-sized pieces, retaining the seeds and skin.
2 Place in a large serving bowl with the garlic clove and torn basil leaves.
3 Drench in olive oil and season with black pepper and a sprinkling of salt flakes.
4 Drain the cooked pasta and pour into the bowl. Mix well and serve immediately, adding more oil and seasoning if required.

RICE CRUDAIOLA

1½ teacups of short-grain
   brown rice
salt
1 small red onion,
   chopped small
5 ounces white tuna in olive oil
1 garlic clove peeled
   and squashed
1 teaspoon harissa paste
juice of 1 lemon
1 ounce torn fresh arugula
   leaves

Rinse the rice and cook in a large pot of boiling salted water. When cooked but still al dente, drain and add this and the other ingredients to the Crudaiola mix above. The oil and the lemon juice will emulsify with the heat of the just-drained rice to create a lightly dressed risotto. Creamy, dreamy, and savory.

TASTY TRANSFORMATIONS

You can experiment adding any of the following, cut in small pieces, and using the same method: chilies, lemon zest, tuna, anchovy, prosciutto crudo or cotto, capers, mozzarella, ricotta, arugula leaves, pesto or tapenade.

THE TOP 10 CLASSIC PASTA SAUCES OF ALL TIME

1 ALFREDO

Alfredo is the king of the fresh pasta sauces and a firm international favorite. This dish can also be de
a 'heart attack on a plate'! Invented in Rome, at a restaurant called Alfredo alla Scrofa (which, incidenta
'at the sow's'), since the 1940s this dish has been the pasta 'pig-out', particularly in the USA, where it is now
transformed with additional ingredients such as shrimp, chicken, garlic, and parsley. This creamy delight was s
by the restaurant owner, Alfredo, with a gold spoon and fork given to him by Douglas Fairbanks and Mary Pickfor
while on their honeymoon in 1927.

Heat 1¼ cups of the cream and all the butter in a heavy-based pan over a medium heat for about 2–3 minutes, stirring occasionally, until the butter has melted into the cream. Stir in the cheese and remove from the heat. Add the drained cooked pasta and toss with the remaining cream and nutmeg. (If the sauce is a little too runny, heat over a low heat until it is thickened.) Season carefully–this dish rarely needs salt as the cheese imparts enough–and serve.

RECOMMENDED PASTA Fettuccine is synonymous with Alfredo all over Italy, but this deliciously rich sauce makes anything it coats wonderful.

1¾ cups heavy cream
½ pound very fresh unsalted butter
5 ounces grated Parmesan cheese or half
  that and half pecorino cheese
pinch of freshly grated nutmeg
salt flakes and white pepper

TASTY TRANSFORMATIONS

AL LIMONE

For a creamy lemon pasta, the juice of 1 lemon and the grated zest of 2 can be added to this dish, together with a handful of chopped flat-leaf parsley. Add the juice in the early stages with the butter and cream. Add the zest and chopped parsley before the tossing.

VARIATIONS For a super-charged Al Limone i Vodka (Lemon & Vodka), proceed as above, adding a splash of vodka to the toss. Heat over a low heat until thickened and vodka has evaporated.
Pasta al Limone can also be made without any cream at all, dressed instead with olive oil, the juice of 2–3 lemons, a couple of handfuls of torn basil leaves and 5 ounces grated Parmesan cheese. Mix the grated zest and juice of the lemons with a generous splash of olive oil, add the Parmesan, and season. Stir into the hot pasta with the basil leaves and plenty of black pepper.

RECOMMENDED PASTA Fettuccine, spaghetti or short pasta shapes

RICH AND FAMOUS

I like to bling up the basic Alfredo and top each serving with a teaspoon of salmon eggs, a pinch of finely chopped chives, ground black pepper and sprinkled gold flake (see page 40). Gold cutlery is optional!

...because it does not deal with the kill—an instinct I have rather hypocritically
...o get clobbered with vertiginous leather heels; today I keep my shoes on and go
...ly as far as the windowsill. I will cook and eat almost anything that is already dead,
...e me a spineless hypocrite or the victim of a common culinary conundrum?

...d the onion, garlic, and chili, if using it.
...nd beginning to color.
...with white wine or brandy, then sprinkle

3 When the wine has ev... ...d the tomatoes and cook for about
10 minutes over a medium heat, until the tomatoes begin to break down.
4 Adjust the seasoning. Add the drained cooked pasta and toss well.
Serve immediately.

NOTE When checking the seasoning, remember that you can always balance
overly acidic tomato with a pinch of sugar.

RECOMMENDED PASTA Spaghetti, linguine

⅔ cup olive oil
1 onion, thinly sliced
3 garlic cloves, thinly sliced
1 fresh chili pepper, seeded,
  or ½ teaspoon chili flakes (optional)
2–3 whole cooked lobsters, each
  about 1 pound, depending on whether
  appetizer or main course
generous splash of dry white wine
  or brandy
handful of fresh flat-leaf parsley, chopped
salt flakes and freshly ground
  black pepper
14 ounces cherry tomatoes, cut in
  half lengthways

TASTY TRANSFORMATION

BLUSHING CHEEKY LOBSTER
Season the lobster sauce above with Rose stardust (page 39) instead of salt
and pepper, and decorate with a very light sprinkling of roughly pounded
rose petals and pink peppercorns for a dish that is truly out of this world.
I would bling this up with gold (page 40) for a meal to clinch the deal!

3 'IN SALSA'—SWEET ONION & ANCHOVY SAUCE

This typically Venetian pasta sauce is served with bigoli, a thick, spaghetti-like pasta with a tiny hole
through the center. Now that you have understood the principles of umami (page 20), I don't have
to tell you what a powerful combination the sweet onion and salty, umami-packed anchovies make.

Heat some oil in a heavy-based pan. Add the onions and cook until golden.
Add the anchovies and black pepper. Stir until the anchovies have dissolved
into the softened onions. Use to dress the drained cooked pasta.

RECOMMENDED PASTA Bigoli, spaghetti

olive oil
2 large onions, thinly sliced
200g anchovies in olive oil, drained
freshly ground black pepper

TASTY TRANSFORMATION
Add some fresh truffle shavings or drizzle over a couple of drops of truffle
oil when serving.

4 CARBONARA SAUCE

It is hardly surprising that out of the top 10 classic pasta sauces of all time over half are packed with umami. This creamy Parmesan and pancetta combination is a worldwide favorite that epitomizes *Easy Tasty Italian*. The umami-packed sauce is also super-quick to make and requires no cooking beyond boiling the pasta.

1 Heat the olive oil in a large frying pan. Add the pancetta and fry until it is browned but not too crisp. Set aside.
2 Place the egg yolks and cheese in a large serving bowl, together with a generous grinding of black pepper. Mix well with a fork.
3 Drain the pasta and add immediately to the cheese-and-egg mixture.
4 Add the pancetta and parsley, and toss thoroughly until all is well mixed and creamy.

NOTES A splash of cream can be added to the egg mixture for an extra-creamy effect. This dish does contain raw egg, which is only slightly cooked by the heat of the pasta, so should thus be avoided by those who are not comfortable eating raw egg with its associated risks.

RECOMMENDED PASTA Tagliatelle, spaghetti

TASTY TRANSFORMATIONS

EGG-FREE CARBONARA + ANYTHING

4 tablespoons olive oil
1 garlic clove, thinly sliced
½ pound artichoke pieces in olive oil, drained and roughly chopped
½ pound mascarpone cheese
1 cup heavy cream
salt flakes and freshly ground black pepper
grated zest of 2 lemons
handful of chopped fresh mint or flat-leaf parsley

1 Heat the oil in a pan over a low heat and add the garlic.
2 As the garlic begins to color, add the artichoke pieces, mascarpone, and cream. Cook on a low heat until slightly reduced and creamy.
3 Season with salt, freshly grated lemon zest, and plenty of black pepper.
4 Sprinkle with the chopped herbs to serve.

VARIATIONS Artichoke pieces can be replaced with ½ pound of any of the Trifolati (page 33). Experiment by adding an extra handful of fresh herbs with the parsley. Try tarragon with mushrooms, mint with zucchini, and artichoke. For U-mamma!, try adding 3 ounces finely chopped prosciutto when heating the garlic, then proceed as above, adding artichoke or basic trifolata, and serve with grated Parmesan cheese.

3 tablespoons olive oil
5 ounces pancetta, cut in strips
4 fresh egg yolks (use only very fresh eggs)
4 tablespoons grated Parmesan cheese
freshly ground black pepper
1 tablespoon chopped fresh
* flat-leaf parsley*

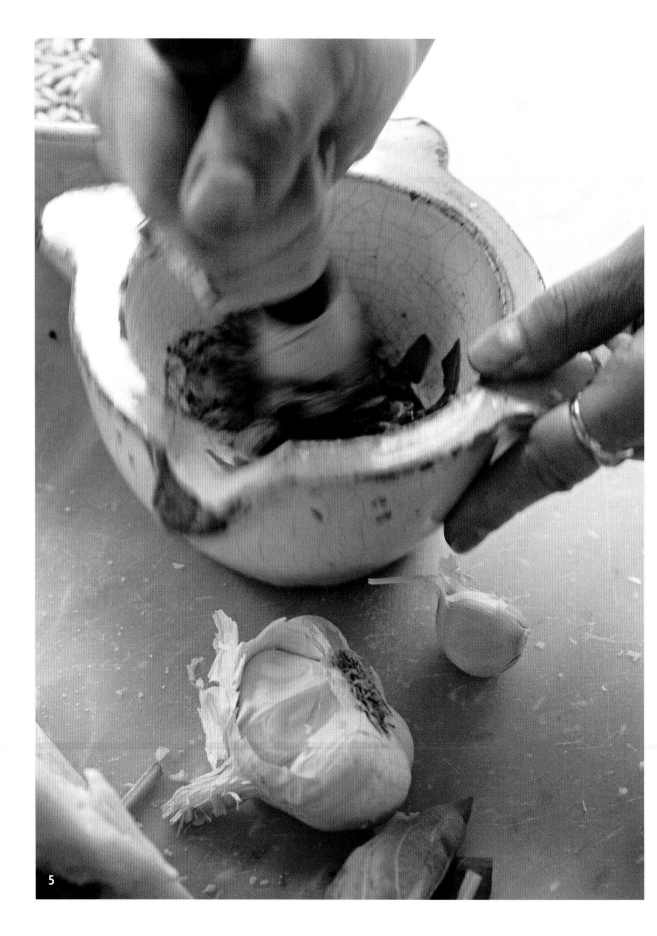

5 PESTO ALLA GENOVESE (CLASSIC GENOVESE PESTO)

This vibrant green sauce captures the flavors of Liguria and is traditionally served with hand-rolled pasta twists called trofie or small linguine called trenette. In Liguria, diced potato and green beans are added to the pasta water towards the end of cooking and drained with the pasta, then toasted pine nuts are scattered on top to serve.

Cook the chosen pasta shape and the potato cubes in plenty of salted boiling water. About 5 minutes before draining, add the green beans. Place the pesto in the bottom of a large serving dish, then add the drained cooked pasta and vegetables, and toss until thoroughly coated, adding some extra olive oil if necessary. Top with scattered toasted pine nuts and torn fresh basil leaves. Serve with grated Parmesan or pecorino.

NOTE If you don't have the time or the energy, you can use any good brand of commercial pesto, of which there are many.

RECOMMENDED PASTA Trofie, trenette, egg pasta, tagliatelle, garganelli

*1 large potato, cut in
  thumbnail-sized dice
7 ounces green beans, trimmed
  and cut in 1-inch-long pieces
Basic pesto (page 29)
extra virgin olive oil
salt flakes and freshly ground
  black pepper
handful of toasted pine nuts
sprig of fresh basil leaves
grated Parmesan or pecorino cheese,
  to serve*

TASTY TRANSFORMATION

CREAMY PESTO WITH ASPARAGUS & CRISPY PANCETTA

*1 garlic clove, split into quarters
7 ounces finely chopped pancetta or bacon
¾ ounce butter
½ cup heavy cream
½ cup Basic pesto (page 29)
10 ounces chopped asparagus (fork-sized pieces about 1 inch long)
salt flakes and freshly ground black pepper
grated zest of 1 lemon (if using dried pasta)
grated Parmesan cheese, to serve*

Fry the garlic and pancetta in the butter. When cooked but not too crisp, add the cream and pesto. Gently heat through and allow to thicken until it coats the back of a spoon. Remove from the heat.

Cook the pasta and asparagus together in a large pot of salted boiling water; the pasta should be al dente and the asparagus vibrant and crisp.

NOTE If using fresh pasta like tagliatelle, then 3 minutes is enough for both; if using dry pasta, add the asparagus to the water 3 minutes before the end of the pasta cooking time. Grate the lemon zest into the bottom of your serving bowl, add the hot drained pasta and asparagus with the pesto sauce. Mix well and serve immediately, with grated Parmesan and plenty of black pepper.

6 NONNA PASQUA'S QUICK RAGÚ

This is my grandmother's recipe and is about as easy and tasty as it gets. Loaded with U-mamma! the seared meat and concentrated tomato, enhanced by the wine and garlic, combine to create a ragú to die for, I have to be careful not to eat it all while 'tasting' for seasoning. It is a meatier olive-oil-based ragú and not the juicy tomato-based bolognaise below.

Heat the oil in a heavy-based saucepan. Add the garlic and onion. When these are sizzling, add the meat and seal it over a moderate-to-high heat until well browned all over. Season and add the bay leaf and tomato paste. Cook on a low heat, stirring regularly to prevent the bottom burning, until the oil begins to separate from the sauce. Add the wine and cook for a further 5 minutes, or until the wine has been absorbed. Serve with plenty of grated Parmesan and black pepper.

RECOMMENDED PASTA I love this sauce with conchiglie (pasta shells) that trap the tasty meat or fusilli, but my kids love it with spaghetti.

TASTY TRANSFORMATION

For a juicy Bolognaise, add two 14-ounce cans of chopped tomato and a pinch of dried oregano. Or better still, add enough soffritto basic sugo (page 84) to give the consistency required. A good-quality tomato pasta sauce from a jar could also be added with excellent results.

NOTE True Bolognaise ragú has many ingredients that make up its magic, starting with 2–3 different chopped meats, chicken livers, and pancetta, all slow-cooked in a soffritto with the addition of both wine and milk. The result is truly delicious, but if my grandmother cut to the chase 75 years ago, I feel it would be rude not to do so today!

5 tablespoons olive oil
1 garlic clove, peeled, squashed, and halved
1 onion, sliced into 8 wedges
1 pound ground beef
salt flakes and freshly ground black pepper
1 large bay leaf
2 ounces (a good squirt or dollop) concentrated tomato paste
1 glass of red or white wine
freshly grated Parmesan, to serve

7 EASY TASTY PUTTANESCA

Puttanesca sauce goes with any short type of pasta, like fusilli, but is also great with spaghetti. The name derives from the Italian for 'whore', and there are many very different theories as to how it got its name ('a whore in the kitchen' indeed).

Heat the oil in a heavy-based saucepan and sauté the garlic and chili until the garlic begins to color. Stir in all the other ingredients and season with black pepper (the olives, capers, and anchovies will probably make it salty enough). Allow to simmer gently on a low heat for about 10–15 minutes, or until the tomatoes begin to break down. If the tomatoes are too acidic, balance with a pinch of sugar.

VARIATIONS I sometimes add a squeeze of lemon juice and some grated zest for a bit of extra zing. For a version without anchovies, crumble in some feta cheese at the last minute.

RECOMMENDED PASTA Spaghetti, tagliatelle, pappardelle

TASTY TRANSFORMATION

EASY TUNNY PUTTANESCA

7-8 ounces tuna in olive oil (preferably white)
splash of white wine
1 tablespoon chopped fresh flat-leaf parsley
large strip of lemon zest

Proceed as above. When the garlic begins to color, add the tuna and douse with a splash of white wine. When that has evaporated, add the parsley and other ingredients as above. Add the lemon zest about 5 minutes before the end of cooking–not before, or it can turn the sauce bitter.

⅔ cup olive oil
4 garlic cloves, thinly sliced
2 fresh red chilies, seeded and finely chopped, or ½ teaspoon chili flakes
1⅓ pounds cherry tomatoes, halved lengthways
4 tablespoons drained and roughly chopped pitted black olives in olive oil (Kalamata or Taggiasche)
2 tablespoons capers, drained
5 anchovies in oil, drained and roughly chopped
handful of fresh basil leaves, torn
salt flakes and freshly ground black pepper

8 VONGOLE SAUCE (CLAM SAUCE)

It is important that the fresh clams are well cleaned before cooking. Rinse them in several changes of water until the water is clear. Then add a handful of sea salt and leave to 'purge' in cold salted water for a few hours. Drain and rinse before using. Sort through the clams, discarding any shells that are open and do not snap shut when tapped, as they are dead and potentially dangerous.

1 Heat some olive oil (¼ inch deep) in a large frying pan that has a lid. Add the sliced garlic and chili, if using it.

2 When the pan is nice and hot, add the clams and cover with the lid. Cook for 5–7 minutes, shaking frequently to help the clams open up.

3 Discard any clams that are still closed and splash the others with ¼ glass of white wine.

4 When the wine has evaporated, add half the chopped parsley and plenty of ground black pepper. As clams are salty by nature, taste the sauce before seasoning further.

5 The spaghetti cooking time should be timed to coincide with the sauce being ready. Drain the spaghetti and toss in the pan with the clams.

6 For a really creamy sauce, add a few spoonfuls of the starchy pasta water to the pan and toss the spaghetti in the sauce with the rest of the parsley. Some indulgent 'cheats' add a tiny bit of butter to achieve this effect. That's OK.

VARIATION In truth, like calves' liver, this is a dish I save to eat in restaurants and one that I cook only when by the sea. Fresh clams can be replaced with two large jars/cans of clams in brine. Drain the clams from the brine and follow the recipe but cook for only 2–3 minutes before splashing with wine. Adding 7 ounces chopped cherry tomatoes after the wine evaporates gives juice and extra flavor when using canned clams.

RECOMMENDED PASTA Spaghetti, linguine

TASTY TRANSFORMATION

ADD TO THE BASE RECIPE ½ teaspoon chili flakes or 1–2 fresh chilies, seeded and finely chopped, with the garlic; or 10 ounces chopped fresh tomato after the wine has evaporated.

olive oil
4 garlic cloves
2 red chilies, seeded (optional)
3½ pounds 'vongole' (fresh, live baby clams)
splash of white wine
large handful of fresh flat-leaf parsley, chopped
salt flakes and freshly ground black pepper

9 AL GRANCHIO (CRAB SAUCE)

Being a Cancerian, I could not sidestep this easy tasty dish. Again, I have cut out the kill as, like lobster, fresh picked crab is now readily available in most supermarkets.

Mix all the ingredients together and season. This is a fairly loose sauce; therefore add extra olive oil if it is too dry and adjust the seasoning. Garnish with chopped parsley. There is no need to cook this sauce–just add the drained cooked pasta to release all the delicate flavors.

RECOMMENDED PASTA Ideal with linguine or tagliolini

TASTY TRANSFORMATION

CRAB TRIFOLATA

For another olive-oil-based sauce, add crab to any of the Trifolati on page 33. Crab is ideally paired with zucchini, artichoke, and asparagus.

7 ounces any trifolata (page 33)
3½ ounces picked cooked white crabmeat
squeeze of lemon juice
chopped fresh flat-leaf parsley
drizzle of olive oil
1 chili, seeded and finely chopped (optional)

Stir the crabmeat into the final stage of the trifolata. Season and serve with a sprinkling of chopped flat-leaf parsley, a squeeze of lemon juice, and a drizzle of olive oil. Chili can be added at the initial stage of the trifolata for extra bite.

7 ounces picked cooked white crabmeat
3½ ounces picked cooked brown crabmeat
generous handful of chopped fresh
* flat-leaf parsley*
⅔ cup extra virgin olive oil
juice and grated zest of 2 lemons
2 garlic cloves, crushed
2 fresh red chilies, seeded and
* finely chopped*
salt flakes and freshly ground
* black pepper*

10 AGLIO E OLIO
(GARLIC & OIL SAUCE: HARDCORE PUNK VERSION)

I named this Hardcore Punk Version because this is the pesto I make when I am inspired by the Beastie Boy's song "I Want Some." Music is as inspirational as food.

1 Heat the oil in a large frying pan. Add the garlic and chili, and a light sprinkling of salt flakes.
2 Cook over a low heat to allow the garlic to flavor the oil. Remove from the heat when the garlic begins to color and slightly puff, taking care not to burn it; otherwise it will taste bitter.
3 Drain the spaghetti and add to the pan. Toss with the chopped herbs, lemon zest, and ground black pepper; if a little dry, add more oil.
4 Serve immediately with grated Parmesan or pecorino cheese.

VARIATION Three chopped anchovies can be added to the garlic-chili mix in the frying pan for extra U-mamma!

RECOMMENDED PASTA Spaghetti or spaghettini

½ cup olive oil
2 heads of garlic, each clove peeled
* and thinly sliced*
2 whole red chilies, thinly sliced
* (for really hot, add some chili flakes too)*
salt flakes and freshly ground black pepper
small handful of fresh basil leaves, chopped
small handful of fresh mint leaves, chopped
large handful of fresh flat-leaf parsley, chopped
grated zest of 2 lemons
grated Parmesan or pecorino cheese,
* to serve*

RISOTTO

A FISTFUL OF PUDDING RICE

Risotto is a literally a meal in the palm of your hand. Combine a fistful of pudding rice with an onion and some tasty stock for yet another dish that is way more than the sum of its parts. The basic principle of risotto is to beat the hell out of a rice kernel so that it releases as much starch as possible without overcooking. The more you stir, the more starch is released; the more starch is released, the creamier the risotto. It is that simple.

HOW TO COOK RISOTTO

The idea is slowly to add hot liquid (usually stock) to the rice and, as the liquid is absorbed and more starch is thrown out through your continuous stirring, the risotto 'grows' into creamy easy tasty comfort food.

As with most dishes, the making of a risotto begins with the softening of some onion in butter or oil. It is very important that the onion is really very finely chopped, as it literally needs to disappear!

Then add the rice and stir it into the oniony butter/oil until all the grains are coated with it and they look translucent and glassy. It is important throughout these early stages that you do not allow the butter/oil to overheat or any of the ingredients to brown, as this will spoil the delicate look and flavor of the risotto.

Then add your flavoring ingredients, i.e. vegetables, fish, etc., unless preparing a simple Parmesan- or booze-based risotto.

Add the wine and cook, stirring with a wooden spoon, until it has all evaporated.

Next, start adding the hot stock, a ladleful at a time, allowing each ladleful to be absorbed before you add the next. Remember, the more you stir, the creamier the risotto. By the time you finish adding the stock, your rice should be soft on the outside with a firm center, and the risotto should be nice and creamy. This will take about 18 minutes. If you run out of stock and your rice is still a bit less than tender, add some hot water.

The final stage of risotto-making is what is called the *mantecatura*; that is, when you make your risotto even more creamy just before serving by removing the pot from the heat and beating in very cold butter and grated cheese. This is considered a great skill in Italy and an important part of making the perfect risotto. It is important that your butter is cold and chopped into little pieces so that it does not split the mixture. Some people cheat, including Italians and chefs, by adding a splash of cream or mascarpone at this point. I personally prefer putting in the elbow grease.

As far as rice species go, I have recommended Arborio rice throughout. It is the perfect rice for risotto and, although less glamorous than some of its trendier relatives, this rice delivers every time. What's not to like?

EASY TASTY BASIC RISOTTO ALLA PARMIGIANA

Prepare both the butter and the cheese for the mantecatura *and keep them in the refrigerator until needed at the end.*

1 In a large heavy-based pan, sauté the onion in the butter or oil until soft.

2 Add the rice and stir in the onion until translucent and glassy. Do not allow the butter to overheat or any of the ingredients to brown.

3 Add the wine and stir well until evaporated.

4 Add a ladleful of hot stock and simmer, stirring all the time with a wooden spoon. As the stock is absorbed, continue to add a ladleful at a time, still stirring. Remember, the more you stir, the creamier the risotto. When all the stock has been incorporated, your rice should be soft on the outside with a firm center, and the risotto should be nice and creamy. This will take about 18 minutes.

5 Remove the pan from the heat and adjust the seasoning (not before, as a flavorful stock may mean you do not need to add salt). Beat in the butter and Parmesan from the refrigerator (the *mantecatura*) and serve immediately.

NOTE For a looser risotto with less bite, add a little extra stock on a high heat so as not to overcook the rice.

TASTY TRANSFORMATION

Use up any leftover gravy by drizzling it over this simple risotto for pure U-mamma! For extra depth, very lightly sprinkle the risotto with Chili chocolate stardust (page 39). I would also mix some gold flakes (page 40) into the stardust.

1 onion, very finely chopped in a food processor to the size of the grains of rice

1 ounce butter (3 tablespoons olive oil can be used instead of the butter)

11 ounces Arborio rice (or 1 fistful per person plus 2 for the pot)

1 glass (½ cup) of dry white wine

4½ cups hot chicken or vegetable stock, or 2 stock cubes dissolved in 4½ cups boiling water

TO FINISH (MANTECATURA)

salt flakes and freshly ground black pepper, if necessary

2 ounces cold butter, cut in small cubes

3 ounces finely grated Parmesan cheese

PESTO & FRESH TOMATO RISOTTO

Add 3–4 tablespoons of fresh pesto at the *mantecatura*. Only add a little of the Parmesan, as it is already in the pesto. Top with a tablespoon of chopped fresh tomato and a basil leaf.

STRAWBERRY RISOTTO

Add 12 ounces roughly chopped strawberries just before the end of cooking. Drizzle with a drop of balsamic vinegar and grind in some black pepper to serve.

RISOTTO ALLA MILANESE (SAFFRON RISOTTO)

This classic Milanese risotto has a Parmigiana base. Proceed as for the basic risotto on the previous page, adding a sachet (about 30 threads) of saffron just after the wine has evaporated. See Osso buco, page 158.

BOOZY RISOTTO

For a boozy base, which can be topped with anything from caviar and mascarpone to thinly sliced truffle and gold (page 40), replace the white wine with your preferred booze at the beginning and half of the last ladleful of stock at the end with either pink or white Champagne, or Barolo or grappa.

ASPARAGUS & ORANGE

*1 pound fresh green asparagus
grated zest of 1 orange*

Cut off the asparagus tips and put to one side; chop the remaining stalks into fingernail-sized pieces, discarding the woody ends. Follow the basic recipe, adding the chopped stalks just after the onion and the tips with the penultimate ladleful of stock, so that they stay bright and crisp. Add the orange zest with the butter and Parmesan at the *mantecatura* stage. This risotto is also delicious topped with a Mascarpone lemon bomb (page 35).

PINK PRAWN & ROSE

*splash of tomato passata
 (a sieved ripe fresh tomato
 can be used)
1 garlic clove, crushed
2 tablespoons brandy or
 vermouth
1 pound peeled raw king
 prawns*

OPTIONAL TOPPING
*Rose stardust (page 39)
1 tablespoon chives, finely
 chopped
4 tablespoons mascarpone*

Add the tomato passata to the (fish) stock to turn it a slightly pink color. Add the garlic with the onion and the brandy or vermouth with the wine. Add the prawns with the penultimate ladleful of stock. Try using the Rose stardust as seasoning at the *mantecatura* stage. As a rule, Parmesan cheese is not added to fish-based pastas or risottos, so just beat in the butter. Serve the risotto topped with a dollop of mascarpone and a sprinkling of chopped chives.

COMPLETE MEAL CHICKEN RISOTTO

Use the leftover chicken and stock from the soup on page 77. Proceed as per the basic recipe, adding the chicken halfway through the cooking, and some shredded kale just before the end.

SAUSAGE & TOMATO RISOTTO

*11 ounces Italian sausages,
 chopped, or diced salami
4 ounces chopped sun-dried
 tomatoes
14-ounce can of chopped plum
 tomatoes
sprig of fresh rosemary*

For this recipe, a thick tomato-and-sausage sauce is made separately, then added to the risotto at the last minute. Sauté half of the onion in a separate pan, add the sausage and cook for 5 minutes, then add both the sun-dried and canned tomatoes, and the rosemary. Season and cook until thickened and tasty.

Or, proceed as per the basic recipe, but using red wine instead of white, and beef stock. Just before the end, stir in the sausage-and-tomato mixture.

Use pecorino cheese instead of Parmesan and add a handful of chopped flat-leaf parsley for the *mantecatura*. Serve with grated pecorino and plenty of black pepper.

OTHER VEGETABLE RISOTTI

Add 14 ounces of any chopped seasonal vegetable to the base recipe after the onions have gone in. There follow some particularly successful ideas, but the possibilities are truly endless. You can also experiment with adding the pastes on page 43. For example, create pure U-mamma! by adding 10 ounces of frozen or fresh peas, half with the onion and half with the penultimate ladleful of stock, and proceed as per the basic recipe. Replace half of the Parmesan in the *mantecatura* with a dollop of the Parmesan and prosciutto paste on page 43.

WILD MUSHROOM & MASCARPONE

Add 14 ounces mixed wild mushrooms (these may need to be sliced, depending on their size) to the butter or oil before the onion and cook until softened, then proceed as before. Finish with the usual *mantecatura* and serve with a dollop of mascarpone on top of each helping, along with a sprinkling of chopped parsley, plenty of black pepper, and a pinch of Wild mushroom & anchovy stardust (page 39).

The mushrooms can either be fresh porcini mushrooms or 2 ounces of dried porcini, reserving the soaking liquid to make up part of the stock. Another option is to use half fresh and half reconstituted dried. Try adding 1 ounce dried porcini (rehydrated as per instructions) to 11 ounces of fresh mixed wild mushrooms.

PUMPKIN & MASCARPONE

1 pound pumpkin
2 sprigs of fresh sage leaves, very finely chopped
4 heaped tablespoons mascarpone
4 small amaretti biscuits (crushed)

Cut the pumpkin into chunks, remove the seeds and roast all but 2 ounces with a little oil, half the sage, and salt and pepper, until soft. When cooked, scoop the pumpkin flesh away from the skin and purée with a hand blender. Add the diced raw pumpkin to the basic risotto base just after the onions. When you are down to adding your penultimate ladleful of stock, also add the purée and proceed as per the basic recipe. Serve with a dollop of mascarpone, a sprinkling of crushed amaretti biscuits, and the remaining sage. For a really fancy finish, fry some extra whole sage leaves in advance and set aside; put one per plate on top of the mascarpone.

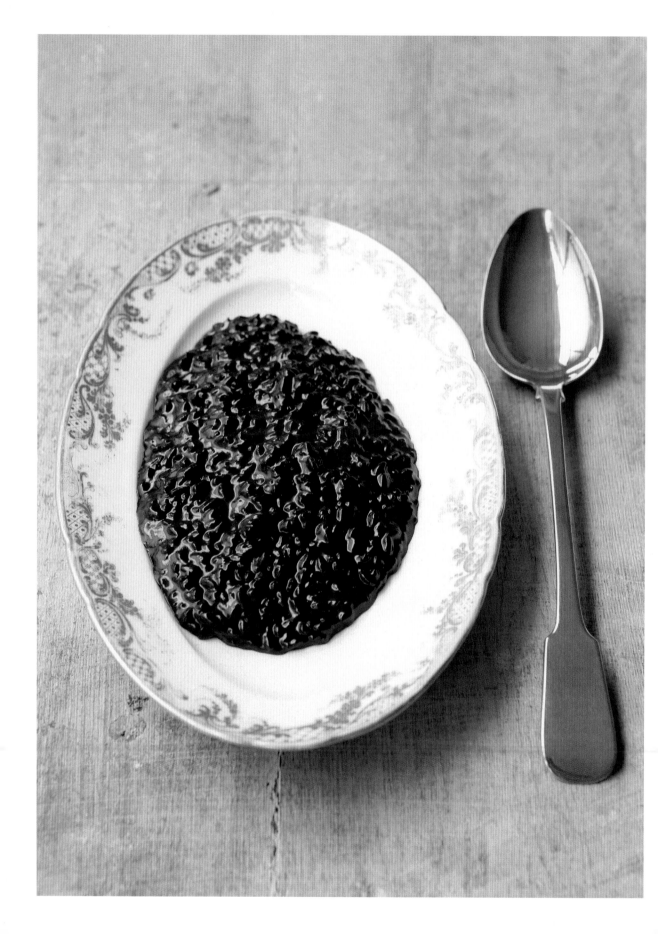

RISOTTO AL NERO DI SEPPIA
(BLACK SQUID INK RISOTTO)

This dish is a total '80s throwback, especially if you add some gold bling (page 40).

1 In a large heavy-based pan, sauté the onion and garlic in the butter or olive oil until soft.

2 Add the rice and stir in the onion until translucent and glassy. Do not allow the butter to overheat or any of the ingredients to brown.

3 Add the squid ink and mix well, then splash with the wine and stir well until the wine has evaporated.

4 Add a ladleful of hot fish stock and the squid ink, and simmer, stirring all the time with a wooden spoon. As the stock is absorbed, continue to add a ladleful at a time, still stirring. Remember, the more you stir, the creamier the risotto! When all the stock has been incorporated, your rice should be soft on the outside with a firm center, and the risotto should be nice and creamy. This will take about 18 minutes.

5 Remove the pan from the heat and adjust the seasoning (not before, as a flavorful stock may mean you do not need to add salt). Beat in the chilled butter for the *mantecatura* and serve immediately.

1 onion, very finely chopped in a food processor to the size of the rice grains
1 garlic clove, peeled and halved
1 ounce butter (3 tablespoons olive oil can be used instead of butter)
11 ounces arborio rice (1 fistful per person plus 2 for the pot)
3 tablespoons squid ink (can be bought in sachets, jars or in powdered form)
1 glass (½ cup) dry white wine
4½ cups hot fish stock, or 2 stock cubes dissolved in 4½ cups boiling water

TO FINISH (MANTECATURA)
salt flakes and freshly ground black pepper, if necessary
2 ounces chilled butter, cut in cubes

POACHING—THE GENTLE ART

When food is poached it is cooked in a liquid, such as water, wine, milk, stock or a court-bouillon as below, that is just simmering very, very gently. Think of the poached egg: it doesn't need the water to be moving too much or it will break up the edges of the white.

VITELLO TONNATO (COLD VEAL IN A TUNA SAUCE)

The sea meets the earth in this popular summer dish. Traditionally made with poached or roasted veal loin, this dish is just as delicious served with more ubiquitous and cheaper cuts of white meat, such as pork or turkey. Indeed, if you're in a real hurry, you can whip up this sauce in a processor and coat ready-cooked white meat, thinly sliced, from the deli or supermarket. The sauce is also great with boiled eggs.

Ensure that as much fat as possible is removed from the meat. Add enough cold water to cover the meat in a saucepan that has a lid. Push the cloves into the onion, and add that to the pot, together with bay leaf, celery, carrot, parsley, salt, and wine. Bring to a boil, add the meat and simmer very gently on a low heat for 1 hour 40 minutes. When cooked, remove the meat from liquid and leave to cool. When cool, slice it thinly across the grain and coat with the Tonnata sauce.

NOTE A winter version of this dish can be made using a simple soffritto (page 84) cut in fingernail-sized pieces, and instead of poaching the loin it can be roasted and splashed with red wine. When cooked, pass the soffritto gravy through a mouli sieve and add it to the mayonnaise and tuna combination. The results many be less delicate, but they are none the less tasty.

SERVES 4–6
*2 pounds veal round (skin and
   fat removed)*
2 cloves
1 onion
1 bay leaf
1 celery rib
1 carrot
2 sprigs of fresh flat-leaf parsley
2 teaspoons salt
splash of white wine
Tonnata sauce (page 27)

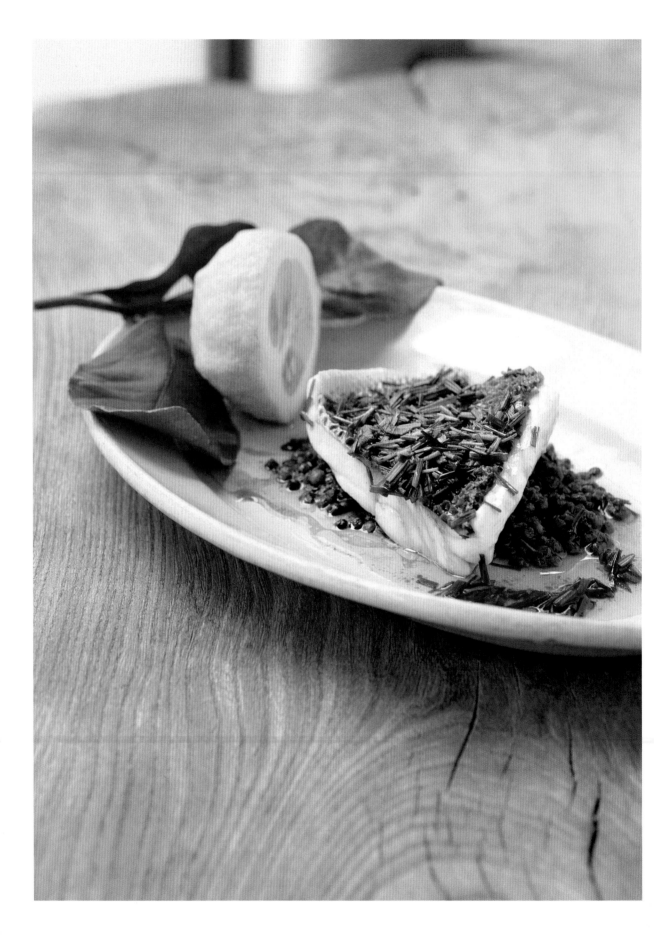

BRANZINO SANTINI (SEA BASS SANTINI)

This lightly poached sea bass with a fresh herb and balsamic dressing is one of my father's signature dishes and a constant favorite at Santini. It is delicious with new potatoes or lentils.

Make the sauce the day before: mix the oil, lemon juice, and balsamic vinegar. Strip the leaves from the rosemary stalk and finely chop all the herbs together. Add these, together with the garlic, to the sauce. Mix in the dissolved Aromat and a generous dash of Worcestershire sauce, then season to taste with salt and pepper. Leave in a cool place for at least 24 hours.

This dish requires the fish to be lightly poached and then dressed with the sauce. Find a large shallow pan or fish kettle in which to poach the fish (something you can easily lift the fish out of without breaking it). Put enough water in the pan to cover the fish, add all poaching liquid ingredients and bring to a boil. Adjust the saltiness, if necessary. When it is boiling, lower the heat to a gentle simmer and place the fish fillets in the water. Poach for about 5 minutes, until the fillets are still firm but cooked and white with no translucency. Carefully remove the fillets from the water and place on a serving plate.

Stir the sauce to mix all ingredients together and spoon over the sea bass.

TASTY TRANSFORMATION

LA GRANDE AGLIATA

This sublimely simple dish is a colorful cornucopia of lightly poached fish, mixed baby vegetables, and soft-cooked eggs. Serve with lashings of Agliata garlic mayonnaise and plenty of lemon wedges for a sharp finish.

2–3 pounds fillets of firm white fish
selection of new/baby vegetables, such as asparagus, carrots,
*   zucchini, new potatoes, green beans, and sprouting broccoli*
Salsa verde (page 31) or Agliata (page 27)
freshly ground black pepper
8 soft-cooked eggs, to serve
lemon wedges, to serve

Use the above poaching recipe to poach the fish lightly. Poach the vegetables separately as their cooking times vary. Accompany the fish and vegetables with homemade Salsa verde or Agliata, plenty of black pepper, the shelled and halved eggs on the plate, and juicy lemon wedges.

SERVES 4
4 large branzino (sea bass) fillets, each
*   about 7–8 ounces*

FOR THE POACHING LIQUID
1 onion, quartered
1 carrot
1 celery rib
½ lemon
splash of white wine
1 bay leaf
1 sprig of fresh parsley
8 black peppercorns
salt

FOR THE SANTINI SAUCE
1 cup extra virgin olive oil
good squeeze of lemon juice
5 tablespoons balsamic vinegar
1 large sprig of fresh rosemary
bunch of fresh chives
bunch of fresh flat-leaf parsley
bunch of fresh sage
2 garlic cloves, very finely chopped
½ teaspoon Aromat seasoning dissolved
*   in 1 tablespoon water*
Worcestershire sauce to taste
salt flakes and freshly ground black
*   pepper*

LUCA LAMARI'S BAGNA CAUDA

This buttery version of a great Piedmontese classic was given to me by a most humble and brilliant 21st-century culinary alchemist, Luca Lamari, a great friend and Executive Chef at Santini. Serve this super-tasty dip with a large bowl of mixed crudités. Bagna cauda makes an alchemic marriage with brassicas: pour it over lightly boiled or steamed romanesco or cauliflower. I also love this rich sauce over grilled steak or lamb.

Half-fill a saucepan with water and bring to a boil. Find a bowl that will hold all your ingredients and is the right size to sit over your saucepan without falling in or sticking out too much. Place the garlic in the bottom of the bowl, top with the anchovies, and finally the butter. Lower the heat and leave to simmer gently until all the ingredients have dissolved into a seriously tasty sauce.

7 ounces garlic, thinly sliced
7 ounces canned anchovies in oil, rinsed and drained
14 ounces unsalted butter

TASTY TRANSFORMATION

This sauce can be transformed by adding some roughly chopped toasted walnuts and a splash of cream. I also grate 100% cacao solids chocolate over it and add a sprinkling of gold (page 40), which is guaranteed to solve all existential problems.

BAGNO-MARIA

The *bagno-maria*, or water bath, most usually known by the French *bain-marie*, is the original transformational tool, the name of which is attributed to Maria Prophetissa, a celebrated third-century alchemist. Mary's bath, as it translates literally, is one of the oldest cooking methods, designed to heat gently and slowly by providing a hot-water barrier between the contents of an inner pot and the direct heat of the flame. The best example of a *bain-marie* is the commonly improvised bowl over a saucepan of boiling water often used for melting chocolate.

One becomes two, two become three, and out of the third comes the one as the fourth. The Axiom of Maria (A metaphorical illustration of the conflict between the conscious and the unconscious, and the journey to a transformed enlightened state. Not as easy as melting chocolate! I find my subconscious often conflicts with my consciousness around the stuff ...)

U-MAMMA! MEATLOAF (POLPETTONE)

Polpettone means 'big meatball' (they can be as big as pies), so the term can be translated, particularly in the USA, as 'meatloaf'—one of my all-time favorite things. The sauce is adapted from a recipe by Anna Del Conte. There is both truth and elegance in Anna's work, which, with her genuine and vast knowledge of Italian food, never cease to inspire me!

Preheat the oven to 375°F. Melt the butter in a frying pan, add the onion and fry until soft and just beginning to color. Splash with the red wine and cook for a couple of seconds over a high heat until the alcohol has evaporated. Place all the other ingredients in a large mixing bowl, add the fried onion mixture, and use your hands to work all the ingredients together rather like a large burger mix. Season but be careful not to add too much salt as the flavors are already fairly salty. As it is inadvisable to eat raw pork, I make a small patty of the mixture and fry it to be able to taste that the seasoning is right. When it is, add the mixture to a buttered 8–9-inch loaf pan.

Place in a deep roasting pan, pour about an inch of boiling water around it from a kettle and cook for 1 hour to 1 hour 20 minutes, until the juices run clear when the center of the mixture is pierced with a skewer. If you see that the top is burning before the loaf is cooked right through, cover it with foil.

NOTE Instead of foil, any leftover prosciutto can be used to protect the top of the meatloaf towards the end of cooking. Some ground meat releases a lot of water; drain this throughout the cooking.

While the meatloaf is in the oven, make the sauce: heat the oil in a heavy-based saucepan, add the onion and garlic, and fry until soft and glassy but not colored. Add the tomatoes and the peppers, breaking the latter up with your hands as you add them. Season and cook on a low heat for 15–20 minutes. When the oil begins to separate from the tomato, blend with a hand blender or in a processor. Return to the pan and add the vinegar, sugar, and cinnamon stick. Season and cook uncovered on a low heat for a further 25 minutes, stirring to prevent sticking and adding a little water if it becomes too thick.

To serve, cover the loaf with a hot serving plate, turn both upside down together, and tap the sides to remove the loaf from the mould. Cut it into slices and serve with the sauce.

TASTY TRANSFORMATION

THE CHEF'S SALTY BALLS

For all you fellow *South Park* fans, the above meatloaf recipe can readily be transformed into tasty little meatballs and shallow-fried. Serve them with drinks on sprigs of rosemary, or add to Tomato sugo (page 84) for spaghetti with meatballs.

3 ounces butter
1 large onion, finely chopped
splash of red wine
1 garlic clove, crushed
7 ounces finely ground beef
7 ounces finely ground pork
7 ounces finely ground veal
3 ounces prosciutto crudo, very finely chopped
1 tablespoon grated Parmesan cheese
2 tablespoons tomato ketchup
1 large egg
3 slices of white bread, ground into bread crumbs in a blender
handful of fresh flat-leaf parsley, finely chopped
sprig of fresh marjoram, finely chopped
salt flakes and freshly ground black pepper

FOR THE RICH TOMATO & RED PEPPER SAUCE
3 tablespoons olive oil
1 onion, finely chopped
2 garlic cloves, peeled and halved
two 14-ounce cans of chopped tomatoes
7 ounces roasted red bell peppers (commercial or fresh)
1 tablespoon red wine vinegar
1 tablespoon superfine sugar
½ cinnamon stick

FIRE
'I was burned'

I. GRILLING

This simple cooking method works on the principle of applying direct or intense radiant heat, where the high temperature causes the surface of the food to caramelize or brown, creating what is called a 'Maillard reaction' which, without going into technical details, is pure umami. Although a very simple and easy cooking method, grilling is one of cooking's quirks, whereby to be able to grill well does, in fact, require considerable skill. It is all about a meat-and-heat affinity in a griddle pan, under a broiler and on the barbecue you are literally playing with fire!

GRILLING

All you need is a good domestic broiler, a cast-iron ridged grilling pan or a barbecue. The recipes in this section are for cooking in the kitchen, but can all be thrown on an outside grill or barbecue. The most common mistakes in grilling are over- or undercooking. Specified cooking times can be misleading and offer a false sense of control, because it really depends on the thickness of the meat or fish, its internal temperature, and how hot the grill is. The following should help you get the right results every time.

STEPS TO GOOD GRILLING

1 Allow the food to come to room temperature before cooking.
2 Brush the food lightly with oil and season it well.
3 Preheat the broiler/grill pan/grill until it is good and hot.
4 Put the food to grill and leave it undisturbed for the right amount of time.
5 Turn it over halfway through to cook the other side. (Although with some thinner fish, you can cook on one side only, particularly if you set it on reflective foil.)
6 Cook the other side undisturbed for the right amount of time.
7 When the food is fully cooked, allow it to rest for 2–3 minutes before serving. This is almost as important here as it is in roasting, as it enhances the internal juiciness of the food.
8 Dress the food with its sauce, condiments, etc. and serve.

To test when food is grilled to perfection, I use my finger; I just prod it to see how it feels:
• If it still feels soft and squidgy, it is still very rare.
• If it is yielding but not too squidgy, it is medium rare.
• If it is firm, it is well-done–or may already be overcooked.

Until you feel confident in using the prod test, you can discreetly cut into the food to see exactly what is going on. Remember, it is always better to undercook red meat than overcook it, as 'past it' really does mean that in this context. Some would recommend a probe thermometer, but to me, seeing that instrument descend upon domestic cookery would be too joyless for words.

As with pasta, always take red meat off the heat just before your preferred state of doneness, as it continues to cook from residual heat while resting. For extra tenderness, leave steaks to stand in a warm oven or on a warm plate for a couple of minutes before serving.

Another tip, especially in the case of grilling fish, is not to flip it too quickly and risk breaking more delicate fillets. If the grill is very hot, as it should be, allow the surface to begin to caramelize rather than attempting to flip too early on, when it is still stuck to the ridges or rack.

NOTE Pork and chicken must be cooked right through. Unless working on a sophisticated outdoor grill like a Weber, it is best to finish off cooking white meats in a preheated hot oven, as it takes a skilled griller to cook joints right through without charring the outside.

RUBS & SEASONINGS
FOR FOOD TO BE GRILLED
Rose stardust, Lavender stardust, Coffee and cardamom stardust, Blackened stardust (page 39)
Salt flakes and freshly ground black pepper

TOPPINGS
Compound butters (page 35, which I sometimes gild, see page 40), Salsas (page 31) and Trifolati (page 33)

BIT ON THE SIDE
Rose chermoula (page 29), Chimichurri (page 29), Salsas (page 31), Horseradish & rose butter (page 35) and Black chocolate elixir (page 45)

For example, take a plain veal or pork chop, seasoned with Lavender stardust, and grill it. Serve with a further sprinkling of stardust, a drizzle of olive oil, and a lemon wedge on the side. Simple yet impressive, this is a truly alchemic dish .

BASIC SALMON 'SANTINI'

Hot carpaccios–oxymoronic but delicious! Both these recipes are my father's and take the principle of the carpaccio a stage further with a quick searing under a hot broiler.

1 salmon fillet, about
1–1¼ pounds
salt flakes and freshly ground
black pepper
extra virgin olive oil
handful of fresh dill
1 tablespoon green peppercorns,
drained
1 tablespoon small capers,
drained and rinsed
1 lemon or lime

1 Using a sharp knife, cut the salmon into thin slices (as if it were smoked salmon). If you can't get them really thin, you can always put them between two pieces of parchment paper and flatten with the heel of your hand.

2 Arrange the slices on an ovenproof serving plate, without overlapping, to cover the entire surface.

3 Season with salt flakes and freshly ground black pepper, drizzle with a little olive oil, and add some sprigs of dill, and a sprinkling of green peppercorns and capers.

4 Leave to stand for 10 minutes so that flavors can socialize. Preheat a hot broiler.

5 Put the plate under the hot broiler for one minute only, so that the salmon is warmed through but not cooked.

6 Sprinkle with lemon juice and serve at once.

VARIATIONS You can season the salmon with coarse Rose stardust (page 39) and scatter with thinly sliced pink grapefruit.

SEARED CARPACCIO BEEF OR VENISON 'SANTINI'

1 packet of wild arugula or
3 medium zucchini
1 ounce butter (if using zucchini)
1¼–1¾ pounds beef or venison
fillet
salt flakes and freshly ground
black pepper
extra virgin olive oil

If using zucchini, cut them into very fine matchsticks using a mandolin grater and sauté in the butter for a minute or two, so they stay bright and retain their bite.

Slice the meat very thinly and pound flat, using plastic wrap and a meat basher or the heel of your hand. Arrange on an ovenproof serving dish to cover it without overlaps. Season with salt and plenty of black pepper, and give it a generous drizzle of oil.

If using arugula, tear it into small pieces and sprinkle over the meat; if using zucchini, scatter over the meat. Place under a preheated hot broiler for one minute, until the fillet is just colored. Serve immediately.

VARIATIONS The zucchini can be replaced with any of the vegetable trifolati on page 33. This dish can also be seasoned with the Black chocolate elixir (page 45). I then sprinkle it with gold (page 40). Try it with coarse Lavender stardust (page 39) and a splash of lemon juice.

ON THE GRIDDLE

The following recipes are cooked on a very hot griddle pan.

LAMB CHOPS WITH U-MAMMA! GRAPES

Mix the lamb with the rosemary, garlic, and a dousing of olive oil. Leave to infuse, ideally overnight. (Literally toss them in a container with the ingredients and leave the flavors to mingle.)

For the U-mamma! grapes, sauté the onion in the butter with the rosemary until soft and golden. Add the meat extract and grapes, and stir together. Splash with the wine and turn up the heat until the alcohol has evaporated, stirring gently. Adjust the seasoning and set aside.

Preheat a griddle pan. Season the chops with salt and freshly ground black pepper, and grill on both sides until cooked to taste: I like my lamb pink in the middle, yielding but not too squidgy! If your grill pan can only take 4 at a time, preheat the oven to a very low heat, so that you can leave the chops in it to rest as you cook the others.

Serve the lamb topped with the grapes.

12 lamb cutlets or chops
¾ ounce fresh rosemary, chopped
3 garlic cloves, peeled and squashed
olive oil

FOR THE U-MAMMA! GRAPES
1 large onion, finely chopped
2½ ounces unsalted butter
3 sprigs of fresh rosemary
1 generous teaspoon yeast extract (such as Marmite or Vegemite) or my Easy Tasty Magic Taste No 5, Umami Paste, or 2 anchovies in oil, drained and finely chopped
1¾ pounds large green seedless grapes, halved
splash of dry white wine
salt flakes and freshly ground black pepper

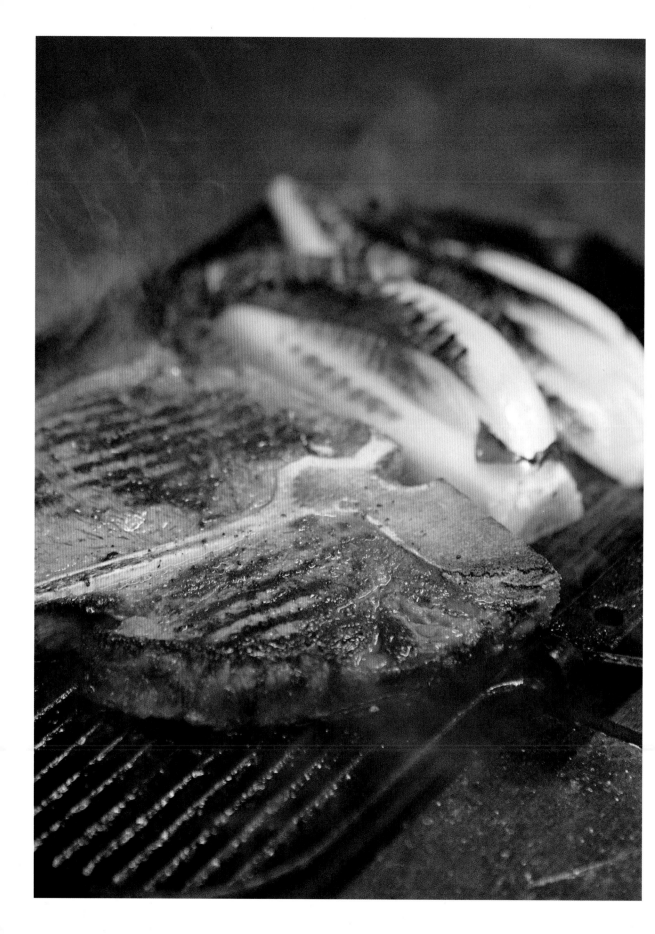

BEEF TAGLIATA WITH RADICCHIO & BLACK CHOCOLATE ELIXIR

Allow the steaks to come to room temperature. Season with salt and pepper and brush with olive oil. Roughly shred the radicchio and lightly sauté it in a little olive oil with the garlic and rosemary. Season with salt and black pepper. Do not overcook, or it will become too limp.

Preheat the griddle pan to a high heat, place the steaks on it and cook both sides to taste. When cooked, leave the meat to rest in a warm place for a couple of minutes, then use a sharp knife to slice it at an angle. If using T-bone, cut the meat away from the bones and then cut into 6-inch slices.

Lay the steak slices overlapping on a plate, season, and top with the sautéed radicchio. Then drizzle with a little extra virgin olive oil and the Black chocolate elixir. Serve immediately with lemon quarters.

VARIATIONS Tagliata is also delicious with a spoonful of one of the vegetable trifolati on page 33. For a creamy pink version of this dish, sauté 2 ounces of pancetta cubes in a little olive oil with some sliced garlic until crisp, add the radicchio and splash with a drop of red wine. When the wine has evaporated, add a cup of heavy cream. Season and reduce until the sauce coats the back of the spoon. Spoon over the steak, or even use this as a pasta sauce.

4 thick sirloin or T-bone steaks
salt flakes and freshly ground
 black pepper
extra virgin olive oil
2 heads of radicchio, roughly chopped
1 garlic clove, peeled and halved
1 small sprig of fresh rosemary
Black chocolate elixir (page 45)
1 lemon, quartered

MARTINO'S COPPIETTE SKEWERS AL MODO ROMANO WITH BITTER ORANGE & RENAISSANCE STARDUST

This is inspired by a recipe belonging to 15th-century cook, Martino de Rossi, from his book, *Libro de Arte Coquinaria* (*The Art Of Cooking*), a work that still remains significant today in terms of having laid the foundations of Italian cookery. This recipe brings together the well-traveled and the somewhat magical flavors of the Renaissance.

To prepare the marinade, pound the coriander and fennel seeds with the salt flakes using a pestle and mortar. Add the oil and mix to a loose paste, then season with pepper. Rub this over the meat cubes and cover with a plate. Leave to marinate in the refrigerator for a few hours, or overnight, with a weight on top of the plate so that the flavors are literally pressed into the meat.

Prepare the skewers by threading a cube of meat, a couple of bacon squares, a piece of onion, half an orange slice, folded, bacon again, a bay leaf, then meat, and so on. Try to get bacon either side of each meat cube as this will prevent them from drying out.

Preheat the oven to 350°F so that, as the kebabs cook, they can be finished off in the oven if necessary. Heat the griddle pan until very hot and cook each skewer on all sides until the meat juices run clear.

Serve with a drizzle of olive oil, a splash of bitter orange juice, and a dusting of Renaissance stardust.

VARIATION When Seville oranges are not in season, add a dash of Angostura bitters and a splash of lemon juice to the juice of a freshly squeezed orange.

*2 pounds pork or veal loin, cut into
  1½-inch cubes*
*14 ounces smoked streaky bacon, cut
  into squares*
2 red onions
1 orange, cut into slices ½ inch thick
bay leaves (preferably fresh, 1 per skewer)

FOR THE MARINADE
1 teaspoon coriander seeds
1 teaspoon fennel seeds
1 teaspoon salt flakes
3 tablespoons olive oil
ground black pepper

TO SERVE
extra virgin olive oil
*splash of bitter orange juice
  (Seville oranges are best)*
Renaissance stardust (page 39)

BLACKENED T-BONE WITH MANGO, MINT, GRAPPA, & LIME SALSA

This recipe is hot off Beelzebub's BBQ and it is devilishly good. I have put quantities as a guideline, but you do not need to be too precise when mixing this. I have also put larger quantities of the rub than needed for one grilling because life really is too short and this mix will keep for up to 3 months in an airtight container.

Remove the steaks from the refrigerator at least half an hour before cooking to allow them to come to room temperature.

Season both sides of the steaks with the Blackened stardust. Heat the grill pan until very hot. When it is, lightly oil the steaks, place on the hot grill and sear on both sides for 3–5 minutes. Keep turning the steaks until cooked to taste.

Drizzle with olive oil and serve with a spoonful of Mango, mint, grappa, and lime salsa, and a lime wedge on the side.

VARIATION I like to do 'grill and gild' blackened steak, where I serve the grilled blackened steak topped with a slice of a compound butter containing caviar and gold, and a sprinkling of very finely chopped parsley.

SERVES 2
2 large T-bone steaks
Blackened stardust (page 39)
olive oil
Mango, mint, grappa, & lime salsa
  (page 31)
1 lime, quartered

GRILLED CRISPY QUAIL WITH STARDUST, POMEGRANATE, & MINT

Serve this with Pinched Persian rice (page 170) and a chopped mixed salad, dressed with lemon juice and olive oil. Mix a tub of Greek yoghurt with some crushed garlic, olive oil, lemon juice, and seasoning. Serve on the side. (I did say I was only half Italian!) I love making rose petal finger bowls to go with this 'finger lickin' good' dish. Half-fill pretty bowls with warm water then add a lemon or lime slice and floating rose petals or jasmine heads, etc.

Well ahead, ideally the night before, spatchcock the quails by cutting out the backbones and squashing the birds flat. Place in a large container with the torn rosemary and sage, garlic, and a dousing of olive oil. Mix all the ingredients together until the birds are well coated, cover with plastic wrap, and leave to marinate, overnight if possible.

Preheat the oven to 350°F. Remove the birds from the marinade and dust off any herbs, etc. Rub them with Rose stardust, or simply season with salt and pepper.

Preheat a griddle pan and, when it is good and hot, cook each quail, skin side down for around 5 minutes, until golden. Then turn them over and cook the other sides for a further 5 minutes. As they come off the grill, place all the quails on a baking tray and finish in the hot oven until crisp but not burnt.

To serve, sprinkle with more Rose stardust, pomegranate seeds, freshly chopped mint, and a drizzle of olive oil. Serve with fresh lime pieces.

VARIATIONS Replace the Rose stardust with Renaissance stardust (page 39), but do not use as a seasoning before cooking, as the sugar will burn. Season with very little salt and pepper, and sprinkle with Renaissance stardust at the end. Add pomegranate, etc., as above. I also like to give it a light dusting of gold and silver (see page 40).

8 quails
small bunch of fresh rosemary
small bunch of fresh sage
5 garlic cloves, peeled and squashed
olive oil
Rose stardust (page 39)
salt flakes and freshly ground
*   black pepper*
seeds from 2 pomegranates
handful of fresh mint, finely chopped
4 limes, halved

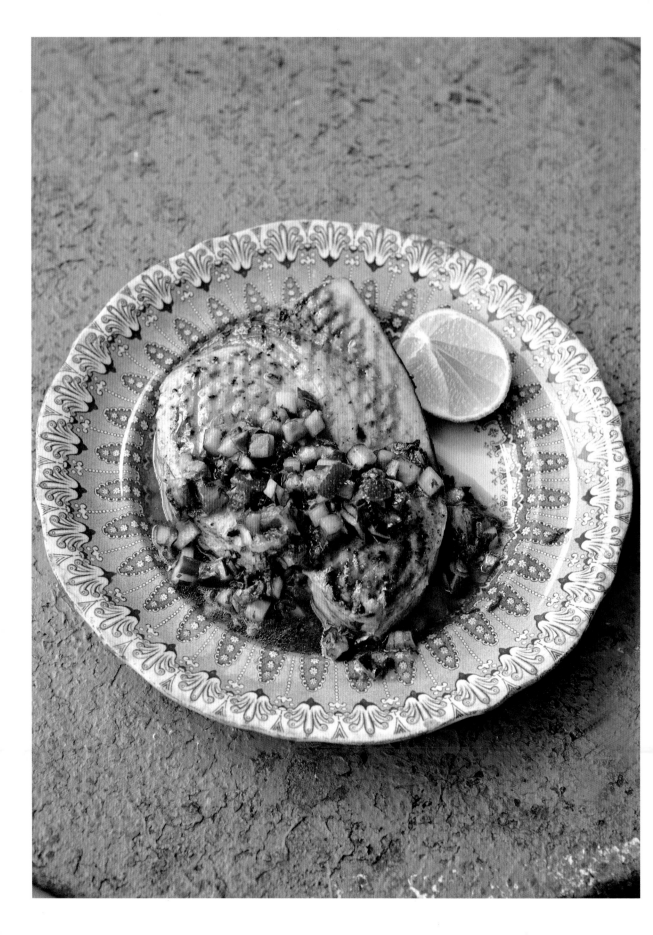

GRILLED SWORDFISH WITH STRAWBERRY, CUCUMBER, & CILANTRO SALSA

If music be the food of love, play on;
Give me excess of it; that surfeiting,
The appetite may sicken, and so die.
WILLIAM SHAKESPEARE
Twelfth Night, ACT I, SCENE I

Heat a griddle pan until very hot. Pat the fish steaks dry with kitchen paper and brush with oil. Season on both sides with salt and pepper (or any other chosen seasoning).

When the grill pan is good and hot, place the fish steaks on it and cook for about 2–4 minutes on each side. For swordfish, I like to cook the steak right through; timing depends on the thickness of the steak.

Remove from the grill and serve with a generous spoonful of the salsa, a drizzle of olive oil, and half a lime.

4 swordfish steaks (do check to ensure
  that the fish is from a sustainable source)
olive oil
salt flakes and freshly ground
  black pepper
Strawberry, cucumber, & cilantro salsa
  (page 31)
2 limes, halved

MONKFISH KEBABS
WITH ROSE CHERMOULA

If using bamboo skewers, remember to soak them in water for a couple of hours to prevent them charring during the cooking. If using long skewers, the ends can be decorated with large rose heads to bring the dish to the table.

To make the marinade, combine the oil, Rose stardust, lime zest, and juice, and pour over the fish cubes. Toss to ensure every piece is coated. Cover and leave to marinate in the refrigerator for 15 minutes.

Thread the fish cubes on skewers. Preheat a griddle pan until hot and lightly cook on all sides until the fish is cooked. Serve with Rose chermoula and lime or lemon wedges.

VARIATION These are also very nice if you alternate the cubes of monkfish with cubes of salmon. Also try replacing the monkfish with tuna if you prefer your fish rare-cooked. Scallops can also be used in this dish.

TASTY WAYS WITH GRILLED FISH

MONKFISH WITH SALSA VERDE (PAGE 31) AND WHOLE LEMON RELISH (PAGE 31)

TUNA WITH WHOLE LEMON RELISH (PAGE 31)

SCALLOP AND PANCETTA SKEWERS WITH SALSA VERDE (PAGE 31)

JUMBO PRAWN SKEWERS WITH SALSA ROSSA (PAGE 31)

800g monkfish fillets, cut into 1½-inch cubes

FOR THE MARINADE
3 tablespoons olive oil
2 teaspoons Rose stardust (page 39) or salt flakes and freshly ground black pepper
grated zest and juice of 1 lime, plus more lime or lemon wedges, to serve
Rose chermoula (page 29)

EASY TASTY CHICKEN

Well ahead, pound the fennel and coriander seeds using a pestle and mortar. To the Basic wet rub, add the lemon juice, pounded seeds, lemon zest, and the chili, if using it. Rub this mixture into the chicken pieces. Leave to marinate in the refrigerator for as long as possible.

Preheat a grill pan and, when very hot, add the chicken pieces and grill both sides for about 10–12 minutes. This dish does cause a lot of smoke, unless you are cooking outside or have major extraction. A way round this is to preheat the oven to 350°F, sear the chicken pieces on both sides on the grill, and then place in a baking tray with the leftover rub, a generous dousing of olive oil, the juice of an extra lemon, and plenty of black pepper. Cook for an extra 20 minutes, or until the meat juices run clear.

Serve scattered with chopped parsley.

VARIATION This is also a wonderful way with a whole spatchcocked chicken in the oven and on the barbecue, or four baby chickens.

1 teaspoon crushed fennel seeds
1 teaspoon crushed coriander seeds
Basic wet rub (page 39)
grated zest and juice of 1 or 2 lemon(s)
½ teaspoon chili flakes (optional)
8 chicken pieces (drumsticks, thighs,
  breasts, etc.)
olive oil (optional)
handful of chopped fresh flat-leaf parsley,
  to serve

I *had a friend who said that if you deep-fried anything it would taste good. I wonder whether, if you took bad love and painted it pink, the same would be true?*

FRYING

Frying – one stop before hell.

Out of the frying pan and into the fire. This cooking method is about as hot as it gets in the kitchen and involves the cooking of food in oil or fat at very high temperatures. Unlike water, fats and oils reach much higher temperatures when heated. This extreme heat causes the sugars on the surface of the food to caramelize, searing the surface and locking in flavor; that's why fried food tastes so good. Of course, this is true to some extent of grilled food, but not quite to the same delicious degree. Temperatures involved in deep-frying are so high that the food needs protecting by a coating, be it a batter or a simple dusting of flour. What you then get is the wonderful contrast of delicious crunchy umami-packed coating and moist perfectly cooked food inside.

Different fats or oils also bring their own flavors to food–for instance, potatoes deep-fried in beef fat are pure umami… That's why you're 'lovin' 'em. Some oils, such as sunflower and peanut, are more suited to high temperatures than others, which can break down. Considering cost and flavor, I recommend olive oil for shallow-frying and a good vegetable oil for deep-frying, where oil can be filtered and stored for use again. When the oil becomes too dark, discard and start again. Remember that in the same way that some oils can flavor foods, they can also readily take on flavors, so if you use oil for frying fish, that oil will add a fishy taste to anything you subsequently fry in it.

To me, there are several different types of frying. In deep-frying, food goes straight to the deep end and cannot touch the bottom. In shallow-frying, food is one- to two-thirds immersed in hot oil. In pan-frying, very little oil is used at all and the food only turned, and in sautéing and stir-frying the food must be moved often to prevent sticking.

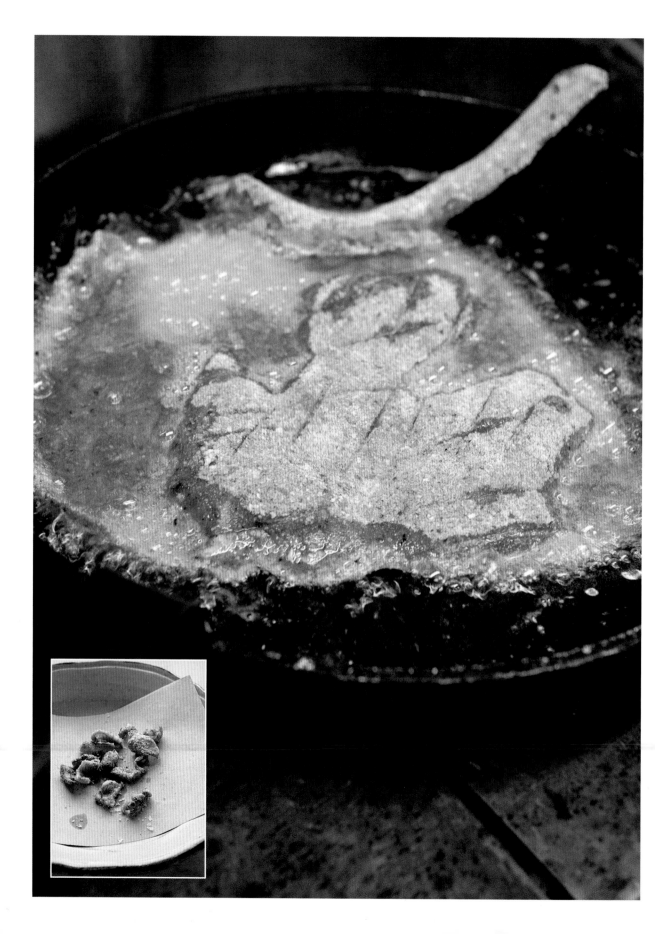

VEAL MILANESE (ELEPHANT EAR)

There are two types of Veal Milanese on the bone: one chunky and the other thin and crisp. For the latter, sandwich each chop between 2 sheets of plastic wrap and flatten gently with a meat hammer or rolling pin until about ¼ inch thick, and looking like an elephant's ear.

1 Prepare 3 large dishes: one containing the flour, one with the beaten egg, and one with the bread crumbs.

2 Heat the butter in a large frying pan.

3 Season both sides of each chop with salt and pepper, and lightly coat them in flour. Dip each in the egg mixture and then into the bread crumbs.

4 Cook the chops, until crisp and golden on both sides. If cooking chunky chops, fry slowly for about 8 minutes on each side to ensure the chop is properly cooked through. (The thinner the chop, the quicker it cooks.)

5 When cooked, remove them from pan and dab with kitchen roll to remove excess fat.

6 Top with a knob of butter and serve with a large lemon wedge. For an extra-professional look, dip a lemon slice in some chopped flat-leaf parsley and hide the butter under it. Serve the wedge on the side all the same.

VARIATION Transform this recipe, replacing the veal chops with chicken fillets, swordfish steaks, or pork chops. Have fun experimenting with crumbs and toppings.

TASTY TRANSFORMATIONS

SUGGESTED TOPPINGS:

VEAL MILANESE CAN BE TOPPED 'VESTITA' WITH A SIMPLE SALSA OF MIXED DICED TOMATO & ARUGULA.
VEAL HOLSTEIN IS TOPPED WITH A FRIED EGG AND SOME ANCHOVIES.
VEAL ALLA PIZZAIOLA IS TOPPED WITH A SPOONFUL OF TOMATO SUGO (PAGE 84), A SLICE OF MOZZARELLA CHEESE AND A PINCH OF OREGANO, THEN FINISHED OFF IN A HOT OVEN TO ALLOW THE CHEESE TO MELT.

CICCIOLE: CRISPY BITS OF HEAVEN

Cut any leftover poultry skin (from around the neck or cavity opening), or some small bits of pork rind, into tiny pieces. Heat some olive oil in a small frying pan and shallow-fry these morsels until really crisp. Drain on kitchen paper and season with a sprinkling of salt (opposite, far left). This is just a greedy treat to use up any bits. There will not be much and you probably will not want to share. Be careful not to burn your tongue!

fistful of plain flour
2 eggs, lightly beaten with a fork
7 ounces dried Basic bread crumbs (see page 47)
2 ounces butter, plus more to serve
salt flakes and freshly ground black pepper
4 large veal chops
lemon wedges, to serve

ZUCCHINI FRITTI (SHOESTRING ZUCCHINI)

These zucchini are ridiculously good and are great served as a hot appetizer with drinks, or as antipasti, or as a side order. I love the umami sprinkle of Parmesan that turns a good dish into a great dish just before serving.

Use a mandolin grater to cut the green outside of the zucchini into julienne strips (the insides can be used in soup). Pour the milk into a large bowl and soak the strips in it.

Mix the flour and cheese, if using it, in a separate bowl and toss the wet zucchini into the flour. Shake well to remove any excess flour. Heat the oil for deep-frying to 375°F and deep-fry the strands in batches until golden brown. Remove and drain on kitchen paper.

Season with a little salt and plenty of ground black pepper.

10 zucchini
3 cups milk
3 ounces plain flour
2 ounces grated Parmesan cheese (optional U-mamma!)
vegetable oil for deep-frying
salt flakes and freshly ground black pepper

FRITTATA

The phrase *girare la frittata*, meaning 'to turn the frittata', is used to describe the action of turning an argument on its side. As sure as eggs is eggs, there are always two sides to a frittata.

Heat 2 tablespoons of the oil in a 10-inch frying pan. When it is hot, add the zucchini, onion, chili (if using it), and garlic, and cook for 5–7 minutes until softened. When the zucchini are beginning to color, add the mint and season with salt and pepper.

Whisk the eggs in a large bowl with the lemon juice, add the cheeses, and pour the mixture over the vegetables in the pan. Cook over a medium heat, stirring gently. When half-cooked, stop stirring, and cook over a lower heat until the underside is solid and well colored.

Oil a large dinner plate, slide the frittata out of the pan on to the plate, and then return to the pan top-side down. Cook until the other side is cooked but the frittata is still soft in the middle.

Serve cut into wedges with a drizzle of oil or some thinly sliced prosciutto. It can be eaten hot or cold.

3 tablespoons olive oil
5 ounces zucchini, thinly sliced (about ½-inch thick)
1 red onion, thinly sliced
½ red chili, deseeded and finely chopped (optional)
1 garlic clove, thinly sliced
1 handful of torn fresh mint leaves
salt flakes and freshly ground black pepper
6 eggs
1 squeeze of lemon juice
7 ounces mature goat cheese
1 handful of grated Parmesan cheese

TASTY TRANSFORMATIONS
The zucchini can be replaced with all sorts of other vegetables, cherry tomatoes, cooked artichoke, mushrooms, fava beans, peas, etc. Herbs and cheeses can change too. Next time you are in Italy, it is worth looking out for a proper frittata pan, a double frying pan that clamps together, making turning the frittata remarkably easy.

IN UMIDO TOP STEW

The stove-top stews that follow epitomize the Easy Tasty principles. They are not sloppy like traditional stews cooked for hours in the oven, but their concentrated sauces, packed with deliciously sticky umami and tender meat, makes them a wonderful and far quicker alternative.

To understand this method of cooking is to open the door to a whole new world of stewing. *Umido* literally means 'damp', 'moist', or 'humid'; therefore, unlike stews where a lot more liquid is required, this stewing method relies on very little moisture, just a glass of wine and perhaps a splash of stock or tomato or lemon juice. Because it is cooked on the hob and not in the oven, after the browning of the meat, the lid is kept tightly on in order to create a 'hothouse' for the stew to cook in without losing any of its moisture.

EASY TASTY BASIC 'IN UMIDO' STEW

1 Heat the olive oil in a wide low pan with a tight-fitting lid. Add the meat or fish and cook briskly until browned on all sides (about 15 minutes for rabbit and chicken, 5–7 minutes for fish, meat, pancetta, and sausage).
2 Add the onion, garlic, rosemary, and parsley (and mushrooms if using them). Season, stir everything together and cook until the onions begin to soften and color.
3 Splash with white wine and cook until the alcohol has evaporated.
4 Then add the tomato in any of the forms indicated, and continue to cook on a low heat with the lid on tightly for about 1 hour 10 minutes. Stir occasionally to prevent sticking, adding a splash of water or stock if it begins to catch.
5 Ideally, serve with polenta.

IN UMIDO EXTRAS

Any of the extras below can be added for extra flavor. Add pancetta and sausage when you add the meat and add the rest after the wine has evaporated. For mushrooms, see the note in step 2, above.

2½ ounces pancetta, cubed
7 ounces green or black olives
6 slices of lemon and the juice of ½ lemon
one of the following herbs: sprig of tarragon,
*   1 bay leaf, 5 sage leaves, handful of basil leaves*
½ pound chopped fresh tomatoes (instead of tomato
*   passata or concentrate)*
4–5 sausages, cut into 1½-inch pieces
7 ounces sliced mushrooms

NOTE Try *in umido* top stews without tomato and an extra splash of wine, lemon juice or stock (or a bit of all three) for deliciously sticky results.

4 tablespoons olive oil
1 whole chicken, cut into pieces or
*   2½–3½ pounds chicken joints*
or
1 whole rabbit, cut into pieces, or
*   2½–3½ pounds rabbit joints*
or
2½ pounds monkfish or eel medallions
*   (or any fish that will hold up when*
*   slow-cooked)*
or
2½ pounds stewing veal, beef, or pork,
*   cut into 1½-inch cubes*
1 onion, sliced
2 garlic cloves, peeled and squashed
2 sprigs of fresh rosemary
handful of chopped fresh flat-leaf parsley
½ cup dry white wine
½ cup tomato passata or 1 tablespoon
*   tomato purée dissolved in ½ cup hot*
*   water, or ½ pound chopped fresh*
*   tomatoes*
½ stock cube (optional) or salt flakes
*   and freshly ground black pepper*

GINO SANTIN'S CARCIOFO SANTINI (AN ARTICHOKE WITH A BIG HEART)

This celebrated dish is all about the power of umami. Created by my father in 1984, Carciofo Santini is his most famous dish, and people book from all over the world to come and eat this total U-mamma! treat. The rich sauce is also served with homemade pappardelle and was Frank Sinatra's favorite. As these artichokes take some time to cook, they are best prepared in advance; they can be reheated gently, adding a ladleful of stock if necessary.

Prepare the artichokes by flattening the tops and cutting off the sharp points of the leaves. Remove the stalks and any tough shabby-looking outer leaves (these can be retained for use in the pasta sauce below). Mix the stock cubes, parsley, garlic, bread crumbs, cheese, salt, and pepper into a powder.

Heat 4 tablespoons of the oil in the base of a pan. When hot but not spitting, put in the artichokes and brown the bottoms, then turn to brown the tops. As they begin to caramelize, do not worry; it is important that they brown as this will only add to the flavor–as long as you do not allow them to burn.

When browned, spread open the leaves of the artichokes and press the powder down into the crevices as far as you can, keeping some back for later. Turn the artichokes upside down (some of the mixture might fall into the bottom of the pan, but this will only help the sauce), set upright again and sprinkle with the remaining powder. Drizzle with more olive oil and add 2 cups of the stock. Bring to a boil and leave to reduce over a low heat. Keep adding stock as the sauce reduces, until the artichokes are tender and the sauce thickens. Cook over a low heat, with the lid on, for about 60-75 minutes. Check regularly to make sure the artichokes don't catch on the bottom and add a ladleful of stock as necessary. Serve the artichokes hot, pouring the pan juices over them. I like to top them with some gold leaf for VIP guests.

NOTE Use the discarded stalks and leaves to make a sauce. Chop the stalks and add them with the leaves to hot oil. When just browning, throw in all the other ingredients and stir well. Add a ladleful of stock and cook slowly, adding stock as necessary. Cook on a low heat with the lid on until the stalks are soft and the gravy is brown. Remove from heat and blend in a food processor, then pass through a mouli sieve for a rich dark sauce. I usually cook this at the same time as the artichokes, keeping some sauce for pasta and adding some to the artichokes for extra dipping.

4 globe artichokes
2 vegetable stock cubes
2 handfuls of fresh flat-leaf parsley, finely chopped
6–8 garlic cloves, finely chopped
3½ ounces bread crumbs
3½ ounces Parmesan cheese, finely grated
salt flakes and freshly ground black pepper
6 tablespoons extra virgin olive oil
4½ cups vegetable stock
edible gold leaf (optional, page 40)

There are three steps to Roll, Wrap, and Splash Heaven, and once mastered there will be no looking back. This umami-filled notion can apply to almost anything and anyone!

ROLL, WRAP, & SPLASH

FISH

Step 1:
ROLL
in grated
Parmesan

Step 2: **WRAP**
in prosciutto

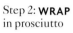

Step 3:
SPLASH
with wine,
stock, etc

*4 pieces of skinned fish
fillet, such as monkfish, cod
loin, sea bass, or swordfish,
each about 150g*

ROLL
*1–2 handfuls of grated
Parmesan cheese
grated zest of ½ lemon
6 fresh sage leaves, chopped
generous grinding of
black pepper*

WRAP
*8 slices of prosciutto crudo
4 whole sage leaves*

SPLASH
*good dousing each of
extra virgin olive oil
and grappa*

Remove the fish from the refrigerator half an
hour before cooking. Preheat the oven
to 400°F.
ROLL each piece in the Parmesan/lemon/
sage/pepper mixture until well coated.
WRAP each in 2 overlapping slices of
prosciutto, tucking a sage leaf inside each
parcel and the prosciutto ends underneath.
Place in a roasting pan.
SPLASH with the oil and add more black
pepper and a sprinkling of salt flakes.
Pop in the oven for 10–20 minutes. Three-
quarters of the way through, SPLASH the
wraps with the grappa. Remove from the
oven when the prosciutto looks dark and
delicious, and the fish is firm to the touch.
NOTES For a glossy sauce, whisk a large
knob of butter into the pan juices. Adjust
the seasoning, pour over the fish, and serve.
If the fish starts looking dry at any point
during cooking, add an extra splash
of grappa. Hic! The prosciutto can be
replaced with strips of smoked salmon.

CHICKEN

4 skinless breasts

ROLL
*1–2 handfuls of grated
Parmesan cheese
sprig of fresh rosemary, chopped
generous grinding of black pepper*

WRAP
*8 slices of prosciutto crudo
4 small sprigs of fresh rosemary*

SPLASH
*good dousing each of extra virgin
olive oil and Marsala or
white wine*

As above, but cook for
20–25 minutes.

ASPARAGUS

*20 long green asparagus stalks,
lightly blanched*

ROLL
*1–2 handfuls of grated
Parmesan cheese
finely grated zest of 1 orange
(retain for juice)
generous grinding of black pepper
drizzle of olive oil*

WRAP
*8 slices of prosciutto crudo
4 orange slices (retain
the rest for juice)*

SPLASH
*good dousing each of
extra virgin olive oil
and Grand Marnier*

As above, but cook for
10–15 minutes.

SCALLOPS

8 shelled king scallops

ROLL
*1–2 handfuls of grated
Parmesan cheese
grated zest of ½ lemon
2 sprigs of fresh flat-leaf parsley,
finely chopped
generous grinding of black pepper*

WRAP
*8 slices of prosciutto crudo
4 small sprigs of fresh lemon thyme*

SPLASH
*good dousing each of
extra virgin olive oil
and Martini Bianco*

As above, but cook for
10–15 minutes.

MOZZARELLA BALLS

12 bocconcini di mozzarella

ROLL
*1–2 handfuls of grated
Parmesan cheese
4 fresh basil leaves, finely chopped
generous grinding of black pepper*

WRAP
12 slices of prosciutto crudo

SPLASH
*good dousing of Tapenade (page 29)
diluted with some extra virgin
olive oil*

As above, but cook for
10–15 minutes.

RuB & RoaSt

BEEF FILLET WITH MASCARPONE & ROSE HORSERADISH

This makes a quick solution for dinner parties or Sunday lunch; experiment with the sauces and salsas in Section 1 (pages 26–31) and the side dishes in the vegetable section (pages 168–173).

1 Add the leaves from 2 sprigs of thyme to the Rose stardust wet rub. Spread the onion wedges and garlic heads in the bottom of the roasting pan, douse with olive oil, and season with salt and pepper and a couple more sprigs of thyme. Place the roasting rack on the top.

2 Pat the fillet dry with some kitchen paper and massage it all over with the wet rub. Leave to stand on the rack in the roasting pan until it is at room temperature, about 20–30 minutes.

3 To prepare the mascarpone and rose horseradish cream, combine all the ingredients, season to taste, and refrigerate.

4 About an hour before you want to serve, preheat the oven to 465°F and position the oven rack at the upper middle level of the oven.

5 When the oven is at temperature, place the fillet in the oven, and cook for 10 minutes.

6 Splash with wine, then reduce the oven temperature to 425°F, and cook for a further 20–25 minutes for medium-rare. If you like your meat medium (check by making a small incision in the centre), leave it in the oven, with it switched off, for a further 10 minutes.

7 When cooked to your taste, remove from the oven, and leave to stand in a warm place for 8 minutes.

8 Place the rested beef on a warmed serving dish and put the roasting pan on the hob. Heat the onion mixture, deglazing the pan with a further splash of wine to make your gravy, scraping up any sediment with a wooden spoon. Season to taste.

9 Serve with the fillet cut into slices about ¼-inch thick, accompanied by the horseradish cream.

NOTE If at any time it looks like the juices in the bottom of the pan are drying up, keep splashing with wine or a little stock.

SERVES 4–6
small bunch of fresh thyme
Rose stardust wet rub (page 39)
2 red onions, each cut into 6 wedges
*2 heads of garlic, cut across
  ½ inch from the top*
olive oil
*salt flakes and freshly ground
  black pepper*
4½ pounds beef fillet, rolled and tied
½ cup rosé wine (or red can be used)

**FOR THE MASCARPONE
& ROSE HORSERADISH CREAM**
6 tablespoons sour cream or crème fraîche
2 tablespoons mascarpone
*2–3 tablespoons prepared grated
  horseradish (fresh or bottled)*
*1 teaspoon dried rose petals (pounded to
  flakes)*
dash of brandy (optional)
pinch of mustard powder (optional)

LAMB FILLET WITH ANCHOVY & HORSERADISH
Rub a lamb fillet with Lavender wet rub (page 39) and replace the rose petals with 1 or 2 pounded anchovies and a little grated orange zest.

U-MAMMA! FILLET
The day before, rub the beef fillet with a paste made of sun-dried tomatoes pounded with grated Parmesan, wrap in prosciutto and tie in place. Leave to marinate overnight and cook as above, splashing with red wine.

VEAL OR PORK FILLET WITH ARTICHOKE & BAY
Cut a pocket across the length of the fillet and fill it with the Artichoke & bay paste (page 43). Roll and tie in place. Rub with salt flakes, black pepper, fresh thyme, bay, and olive oil Cook as above, splash with

white wine during cooking. For extra flavor, wrap in prosciutto or pancetta.
NOTE Any of the pastes on page 43 can be used to fill pockets in this way. If using Chili chocolate wine paste, blend 1 tablespoon of the mix with a handful each of stoned prunes and almonds.

ROSTICCIANA: MOCHA CHILI RIBS

Eve to Adam: 'Is that a spare rib under that fig leaf, or are you just pleased to see me?'

Coffee-rubbed ribs are a cowboy favorite. In the spirit of the great Sergio Leone and his remarkable spaghetti westerns I have combined Italian espresso coffee with the Wild West and put the ciao into chaps. Yeehaw!

1 Make the marinade well ahead, preferably the night before: mix all the ingredients together in a small heavy-based pan and bring to a boil over a high heat. Turn the heat right down and simmer for 15–20 minutes. Remove from heat and leave to cool. Blend.

2 When the marinade is totally cool, place the ribs in a shallow dish, add the marinade and make sure each rib is well coated. Leave to marinate in the refrigerator for at least a couple of hours, preferably overnight, turning occasionally to make sure all the flavors sink in.

3 Bring the ribs back to room temperature before cooking. Preheat the oven to 350°F and spread the ribs across a shallow roasting tray, leaving surplus marinade in the dish.

4 Roast for 30 minutes. Place the leftover marinade in a pan and bring to a boil.

5 When the ribs are browned, sizzling, and cooked right through, remove from the oven and drain any fat from the pan. Pour the remaining marinade over the ribs and mix well. Return to the oven and cook for a further 20 minutes.

NOTE If at any time the ribs look as if they are burning, cover with foil but remember to give them the final blast uncovered; otherwise they will be soggy and not finger-lickin'.

6 Before serving, test that the ribs are cooked right through to the bone–there should be no pink meat.

7 Serve on a large platter topped with Chocolate chili stardust. I also like to give them a sprinkling of gold for special occasions.

VARIATION For a simpler option, double the marinade on page 126 and proceed as above, cooking for 30 minutes, then draining and adding the rest of the marinade, and cooking further. Since this is a drier version, keep draining as necessary to ensure the ribs are crisp and tasty.

SERVES 2
4 pounds pork spare ribs

**FOR THE MOCHA CHILI
BARBECUE MARINADE**
½ cup strong-brewed espresso coffee
½ cup balsamic vinegar
½ cup runny honey
1 cup tomato ketchup
2 tablespoons Dijon mustard
2 tablespoons ground cumin
1 tablespoon grated 100% cacao chocolate
*1 teaspoon chili flakes, or more if looking
   for real heat*
1 tablespoon Worcestershire sauce
1 tablespoon water

TO SERVE
Chocolate chili stardust (page 39)
sprinkling of gold (optional, page 40)

CHOP, CHUCK, & DOUSE

NO-FUSS ROASTED SEA BREAM

These recipes are so simple and so delicious that, once you have made them, you will never need to look at the recipe again. The possibility to experiment with other ingredients is endless. The secret is not to alter the oil or juice levels, so that you still get the saucy bit on the side. I have given these quantities as a guide, but I never really measure anything; I just chop, chuck, and douse it all in. Ask your fishmonger to clean and prepare the fish.

1 Preheat the oven to 350°F.

2 Place both fish in a large roasting tray and stuff each belly with a round of onion, a lemon slice, and a sprig of parsley.

3 Scatter the potato, onions, garlic, cherry tomatoes, olives, capers, anchovies, chopped parsley, and dill sprigs around the fish. Generously douse the fish and vegetables with olive oil, season with salt and pepper, and add the juice of the 3 lemons, throwing in two of the spent halves. Use your hands to mix all the vegetables together around the fish. Do not cover the fish in the vegetables but leave them around the sides.

4 Place in the oven and cook for around 20–25 minutes, or until the potatoes are cooked and crisp in parts, and the tomatoes and onions are soft and saucy.

NOTE If you use enough oil, this dish should not dry out and cause the vegetables to stick or burn. Take care not to let this happen because this is your sauce. If you see that this could be likely, add a dash more oil and a splash of white wine.

ROASTED SEA BREAM WITH BLACK OLIVE, FENNEL, & ORANGE

Replace the capers and tomatoes with potatoes and sliced fennel bulbs, together with the segments from 2 oranges plus the juice of a third. Use only 1 lemon and plenty of dill.

2 sea bream, each about 1-1¼ pounds, scaled and gutted

2 rounds from a large onion (use a separate onion from that below)

3 unwaxed lemons

2 sprigs of fresh flat-leaf parsley

3 large potatoes, cut into discs about ¼ inch thick

3 large red onions, cut into slices ½ inch thick

4 garlic cloves, thinly sliced

1¼ pounds cherry tomatoes, halved lengthways

2 tablespoons black olives in oil (Taggiascha or Kalamata)

1 tablespoon capers, drained and rinsed

3 anchovies in oil, drained and roughly chopped (optional)

1 whole bunch (¾ ounce) fresh flat-leaf parsley, chopped

handful of chopped fresh dill

⅔ cup olive oil

salt flakes and freshly ground black pepper

ROASTED LAMB WITH TOMATO AND PECORINO

1 Preheat the oven to 350°F.

2 Place all the ingredients, except the cheese, oil, lemons, and mint, flat in a large roasting pan. Generously douse in olive oil and lemon juice, season with salt and pepper, and mix together well with your hands. Sprinkle with pecorino cheese and splash with oil.

3 Bake in the oven for about 1 hour 20 minutes. During cooking you can baste with a splash of wine (red or white) and/or a splash of stock. If the meat looks as if it is burning at any time, cover it with foil.

4 Serve sprinkled with the mint.

VARIATION 2 or 3 chopped anchovies and/or a handful of black olives can be added for extra flavor.

SERVES 4–6

2 pounds lean lamb shoulder on the bone, cut large 3-inch pieces

3–4 large potatoes, cut into chunks for roasting

1 pound ripe tomatoes, deseeded and chopped

1 tablespoon fennel seeds

2 red onions, sliced

1 celery rib, sliced

3 garlic cloves, thinly sliced

handful of chopped fresh flat-leaf parsley

sprig of fresh rosemary (leaves only)

handful of chopped fresh oregano

salt flakes and freshly ground black pepper

2 ounces pecorino cheese, finely grated

½ cup olive oil

juice and a piece of zest from 2 lemons

handful of chopped fresh mint, to serve

EARTH

'I am tasty'

SLOW COOKING

Life is too short to slow cook for 4 people, and to stop you wishing you had made more for tomorrow. All these dishes serve 4–6 unless otherwise stated.

The essential tool for this sort of cooking is a large heavy-bottomed cast-iron casserole with a tight-fitting ovenproof lid.

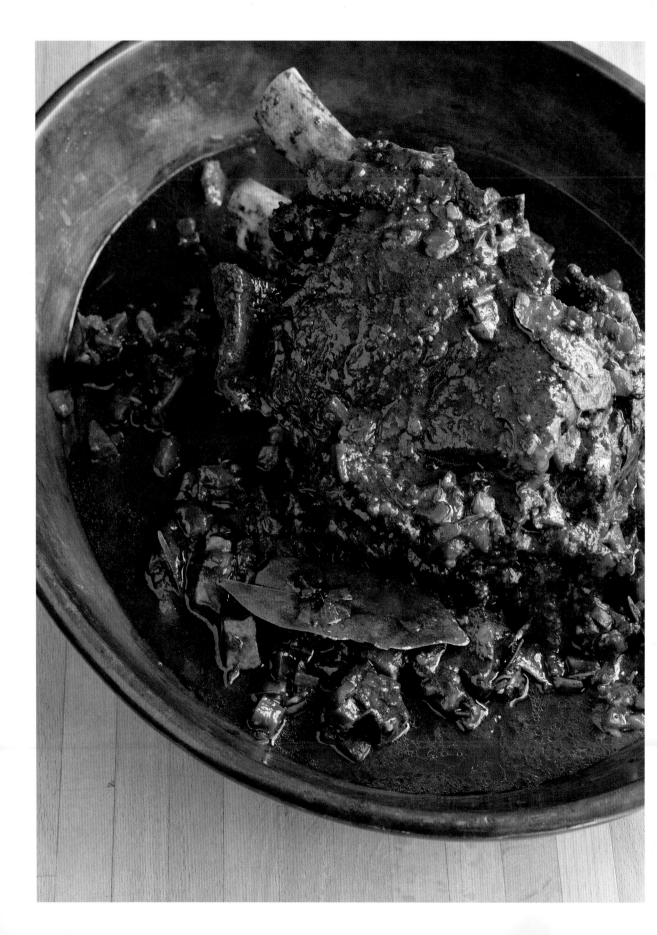

RIB OF BEEF AL BAROLO

I have adapted this recipe from Ada Boni's *The Talisman Italian Cook Book*. I noticed that Elizabeth David had done the same in *Italian Food*. I must point out, though, that, having tested it, the idea of being able to spoon the meat at the end of cooking as they describe in these recipes is never going to happen using a rib roast, as the meat is too lean. I love this recipe with the rib roast but if you want to be able to 'spoon' the meat, swap it for 4–5 pounds of rump or round roast. With much respect to the ladies above, this is my adaptation.

This dish has a 24-hour run-up and requires a large cooking pot with a lid, preferably cast iron.

Make a marinade by mixing the wine, carrot, celery, onion, garlic, bay leaf, and peppercorns (no salt) and pour this over the beef. Leave to marinate for 24 hours in the refrigerator, turning when you remember.

To cook, remove the meat from the marinade, reserving it, and thoroughly pat dry with kitchen paper. Heat the oil in the pot, add the beef and brown on all sides. When browned, season the beef and remove from the pan.

Sauté the lardons and garlic in the hot pot and get them sizzling. Just as they begin to color, deglaze the pan with a ladleful of marinade. Return the beef to the pot and season again. Pour the marinade over the meat and add the chopped tomatoes, anchovies, orange peel, stock cubes, and rosemary. Simmer gently over a very low heat, with the lid tightly on, for a couple of hours, or until the meat is tender. Turn occasionally during cooking to make sure all sides get immersed in the sauce. If it looks like the meat is catching, add a splash of beef stock or, if really indulgent, a drop more wine. Likewise, if at the end of cooking your sauce is too liquid, remove the meat and reduce the sauce over a low heat with the lid off until you have the thick consistency you require.

Serve with creamy mashed potatoes or polenta.

VARIATION Try bombing this rich dish with 1 teaspoon of Chili chocolate wine paste (page 43).

4-5 pounds beef rib roast (tied)
4 tablespoons olive oil
salt flakes and freshly ground
   black pepper
5 ounces pancetta or bacon lardons
2 whole garlic cloves, peeled
two 14-ounce cans of chopped tomatoes
3 canned anchovies in oil, drained
3 large pieces of orange peel
2 beef stock cubes, crumbled
1 sprig of fresh rosemary

FOR THE MARINADE
1 bottle of Barolo or any good
   robust red wine
2 large carrots, sliced
2 celery stalks, sliced
1 large Spanish onion, chopped
3 whole garlic cloves, peeled
1 large bay leaf
4 black peppercorns

GIUSEPPE ROSSELLI'S CARROT & ORANGE OSSO BUCO ALLA MILANESE

Giuseppe has been working as a chef with my father for nearly thirty years, and his hard work and dedication have contributed hugely to the success of Santini. He has a knack for all things tasty and his tangy take on this classic is the best I have ever eaten. The way the orange-infused sauce mingles with the creamy saffron risotto is an indelible food memory etched on my palate.

Like many slow-cooked things, osso buco is always better the next day. I make mine in advance and reheat, adding a tiny splash of stock to loosen it.

Make the soffritto base: put the carrots, onions, garlic, celery, and orange zest in a food processor and blend until the size of grains of pudding rice. Heat the oil in a large sauté pan and add the soffritto base, then fry until the onion goes glassy and begins to soften. Add the white wine, passata, and stock, and leave to cook, uncovered, over a low heat.

Flour the osso buchi on both sides and season with salt and pepper. Heat the olive oil in the casserole and brown the osso buchi on both sides. Remove from the pan and drain on kitchen paper, making sure there is no oil.

Wipe out the inside of the casserole, put the osso buchi back and cover with the reduced sauce from the pan. Cover and cook for 1 hour to 1 hour 30 minutes, until the meat is nice and tender.

Meanwhile, make the gremolata by mixing the ingredients together.

Serve the osso buchi with Risotto alla Milanese (page 104) and top with the Gremolata.

VARIATION Try bombing with a drizzle of Red pepper & orange oil (page 45).

SERVES 6
1 bottle of dry white wine
1 litre tomato passata
1 beef stock cube, dissolved in 1 cup
   hot water
plain flour, to dust
6 osso buchi (veal shins)
salt flakes and freshly ground
   black pepper
4 tablespoons olive oil

FOR THE SOFFRITTO BASE
5 pounds carrots, chopped into chunks
2 large Spanish onions, quartered
4 garlic cloves
1 head of celery, outer leaves removed,
   the rest chopped into large pieces
grated zest of 1 large orange
3 tablespoons olive oil

GREMOLATA, TO SERVE
(The orange is not traditional but I love it.)
handful of chopped fresh flat-leaf parsley
1 garlic clove, very finely chopped
grated zest of ½ lemon
grated zest of ½ orange

VENISON STEW WITH BEETS, JUNIPER, & GRAPPA

For an Anglo-Italian alliance, this stew is wonderful served with creamy mashed potato or a crusty loaf, pickled walnuts and redcurrant jelly on the side.

The day before, place all of the marinade ingredients in a large bowl and mix, then add the venison chunks, mix in well, and cover. Leave to marinate in the refrigerator for 24 hours, turning when you remember.

When ready to cook, remove the venison from the liquid using a slotted spoon, and set the marinade aside for later. Pat the venison dry with kitchen paper. Pour olive oil to cover the bottom of your casserole and add the venison in batches to brown the pieces all over.

Return all the venison to the pan and add the pancetta. When the pancetta begins to color, deglaze the pan with the grappa. When the alcohol has evaporated, sprinkle the contents of the pan with the flour and cook, stirring, for 2 minutes.

Add the reserved marinade, a cup of the stock, and the tomato purée. Cover and simmer over a low heat for around 1 hour 30 minutes, adding more stock if it begins to look dry at any time. When the venison is soft and tender, stir and adjust the seasoning.

Serve with a dollop of crème fraîche on the top and a good sprinkling of chopped herbs.

5 pounds venison, cut into chunks
  for stewing
olive oil
2 ounces pancetta, cubed
½ cup grappa
2 ounces plain flour
4½ cups beef stock
1 tablespoon tomato paste

FOR THE MARINADE
1 bottle of red wine
15 juniper berries, crushed
7 cloves
3 medium shallots, finely chopped
1 pinch of myrtle leaves or 3 bay leaves
½ teaspoon ground cinnamon
3 garlic cloves, squashed
6 medium beets, cut into 1-inch cubes
2 celery ribs, finely chopped
3 sprigs of fresh thyme, leaves only
1 teaspoon cracked peppercorns
pinch of salt flakes

TO SERVE
1 cup crème fraîche
handful of chopped fresh flat-leaf parsley
  and fresh chives mixed

LEG-OVER LAMB

So-called because, with a cooking time of 6 hours, you have plenty of time to do all sorts of things, like drink coffee and read the Sunday papers . . .

Preheat the oven to 250°F. Make slits in the lamb all over, and stuff each hole with a piece of garlic, a piece of anchovy if using it, and some rosemary, pushing them right in with your finger.

Heat the olive oil in a large casserole, add the lamb, and brown it well on all sides. Season with salt and pepper, and add the onions, red wine, and port. Mix the herb jelly, balsamic vinegar, and fresh herbs together, and spoon over the lamb. Cover with a tight-fitting lid and cook in the oven for around 5–6 hours, until the meat is falling off the bone.

VARIATION Bomb the sauce with a teaspoon of Rose, pomegranate, & mint paste (page 43).

5-pound leg of lamb
4 garlic cloves, each cut into 3
3 anchovies in oil (optional), drained and each cut into 4 pieces
2 sprigs of fresh rosemary, cut into 1-inch lengths
3 tablespoons olive oil
salt flakes and freshly ground black pepper
4 red onions, cut into quarters
1½ cups red wine
½ cup port (if you don't have any, increase the wine to 2 cups)
1–2 tablespoons herb or berry jelly (mint, rosemary, redcurrant, sage)
1 tablespoon balsamic vinegar (thick type)
1 tablespoon chopped fresh rosemary
1 tablespoon chopped fresh sage
1 tablespoon chopped fresh mint

36-CLOVE SPRING CHICKEN

This dish was inspired by 16th- and 17th-century Italian recipes, which often use citrus fruit unpeeled, a reminder that the combination of sour pulp, bitter pith, and aromatic peel are all essential to the enjoyment of the fruit, cooked or raw. The transformation of the combative garlic into a soft bitter-sweet accent to the chicken is magical. This recipe was given to me by my Yorkshire granny, Gillian Riley, who adopted me at the tender age of thirty-six. I've been thirty-six ever since …

Preheat the oven to 350°F. Fry the chicken pieces quickly in the oil in a heavy casserole. When they are nice and golden, take them out and turn the garlic cloves over in the casserole.

Put the chicken pieces back on top of the garlic, strew with the bay leaves, olives, and salt and pepper to taste. Tuck the cinnamon stick among the chicken pieces and splash over the white wine. Lay the lemon slices over the chicken, and sprinkle with a pinch of salt and a teaspoon of sugar.

Cover and cook for about 1½ hours in the preheated oven, until the chicken is really tender and the garlic cloves nice and soft, ready to pop out of their (by now fragile) skins.

VARIATION I have often bombed this perfect dish with the Artichoke & bay paste (page 43).

NOTE This is the only recipe in this section that does not feed 6–8, if you need to do that, do the math for 72–CLOVE SPRING CHICKEN!

SERVES 4

1 medium-size chicken, cut into pieces
olive oil for frying
3–4 heads of garlic (about 30–40 cloves), unpeeled
5 bay leaves
5 ounces green olives
salt flakes and freshly ground black pepper
½ cinnamon stick
½ cup white wine
1 large organic unwaxed lemon, as fragrant as possible, unpeeled and thinly sliced
1 teaspoon sugar

MELANZANE ALLA PARMIGIANA (BIG PURPLE TEARDROPS WITH SWEET TOMATOES & BITTER CHOCOLATE)

Eggplant and chocolate have a history together in southern Italian cookery.

Eggplant tastes better once it has been purged of its bitter juices. To this end, layer the slices in a colander, generously sprinkling with salt as you layer. Cover with a plate and press down with a heavy weight. Some Italian cookery books refer to this as leaving the eggplants 'to cry'. Place a plate under the colander and leave to stand for around half an hour until their bitter tears have been collected.

While the eggplant cries, preheat the oven to 400°F and prepare the Fresh tomato & basil sauce.

Rinse the eggplant slices and dry thoroughly with kitchen paper, then flour both sides of each slice. Heat about 1½ inches of olive oil in a large frying pan until really hot, dip a corner of a slice in the oil to test if it sizzles around it. When the oil is ready, add the floured eggplant slices and fry until golden, turning only once (you may have to do this in batches). Remove with a slotted spoon and drain on paper towel.

Butter a large ovenproof dish, cover the bottom with a layer of eggplant slices, spread with a layer of tomato sauce and a sprinkling of grated chocolate, scatter with pieces of chopped mozzarella, some crumbled ricotta, a sprinkling of Parmesan, and some torn basil; repeat until you end with a layer of tomato. Sprinkle with the remaining cheese, grated chocolate, and a drizzle of olive oil.

Bake in the oven for around 35–40 minutes. If the eggplant throws out a lot of excess liquid during cooking, carefully spoon it off, otherwise the dish will be too sloppy.

I prefer to serve this dish once it has cooled down a little.

VARIATION Try bombing with a drizzle of Black chocolate elixir (page 45).

5 eggplants, cut top to bottom in ¼-inch slices
salt flakes and freshly ground black pepper
Fresh tomato & basil sauce (page 86)
plain flour for dusting
olive oil, for frying and finishing
butter, for greasing
2–3 tablespoons 100% cacao chocolate, finely grated
2 large balls of mozzarella, thinly sliced
3 ounces ricotta
5 ounces Parmesan cheese, finely grated
1 handful of fresh basil leaves

Italians tend to treat vegetables like salad, and butter is seldom, if ever, used to dress veg. Instead, Italians boil or steam their vegetables to a point where they are rather overdone for modern tastes, and then drench them in extra virgin olive oil and vinegar or lemon juice. I never depart from this tradition and use a good oil and a slightly sweet Muscat vinegar. Visiting children always eat all their vegetables at my house, much to their mothers' amazement! All these side dishes serve 4.

THE TOP 10 ITALIAN VEGETABLE DISHES

1 MAGIC PINK BROCCOLI

I discovered this truly alchemical dish by pure chance. I simply dressed some steamed purple sprouting broccoli with olive oil and freshly squeezed lemon juice and then went to answer the telephone. When I came back there was a fuchsia moat around these bright green stems. A simple kitchen miracle performed in a moment.

Steam the broccoli until bright and just tender. I prefer it still just a little al dente, but cook it to your taste.

Drain and dress immediately with the olive oil, freshly squeezed lemon juice, salt, and pepper.

TASTY TRANSFORMATIONS
Apply this to any other vegetable you fancy (but you will not get the pink effect). Try boiled potatoes dressed while still hot with plenty of olive oil, a couple of halved garlic cloves, salt and pepper, and a handful of chopped flat-leaf parsley. Mix well and serve with grilled fish.

1 pound purple sprouting broccoli
extra virgin olive oil
juice of 1 lemon
salt flakes and freshly ground black
* pepper*

2 SWEET LAVENDER PARSNIPS

Dilly-dilly delicious . . .

Preheat the oven to 350°F. Place the parsnips in a roasting pan, douse in olive oil and maple syrup, season, and sprinkle with the lavender and thyme. Mix well to make sure each piece is evenly coated. Roast until sticky and golden, about 30–40 minutes.

TASTY TRANSFORMATIONS
I have made this recipe with a selection of roasted vegetables, adding, pumpkin, garlic, sweet potatoes, and red onion, etc. Try drizzling them with balsamic vinegar for a sweet-sour balance.

2 pounds parsnips, cut lengthways into halves
* or quarters, depending on size*
olive oil
5 tablespoons maple syrup
salt flakes and freshly ground black pepper
½ teaspoon dried lavender flowers
3 sprigs of fresh thyme

3 MASHED POTATOES WITH MASCARPONE & SWEET ROASTED GARLIC

I make a venison cottage pie with juniper, myrtle, red wine, and lots of Oxo beef stock cubes, and this mash on top takes a simple pie to the sky and beyond.

Preheat the oven to 350°F and roast the whole garlic head until soft and caramelized but not burnt, about 30–40 minutes.

Boil or steam the potatoes (if boiling, salt the water; if steaming, salt the potatoes) well as, if underdone, you won't get a smooth finish. When cooked, drain if necessary, and return to the pan or put in a food processor. If returning the potatoes to the pan, you will need a hand whisk to beat in the milk, butter and mascarpone, otherwise throw everything together into the processor. More milk or cream can be added to achieve the required consistency of fluffy potato clouds that hold a soft shape. Season with salt, pepper, and a grating of nutmeg.

Remove the garlic cloves from their skins and push the garlic into the hot mash, with random dollops of mascarpone. For an extra dimension, sprinkle with Wild mushroom & anchovy stardust (page 39).

TASTY TRANSFORMATIONS
This treatment also suits other root veg: try it with celery root, or an equal mix of celery root and potato, or make a pink mash with beets or an orange one with rutabaga and/or turnip.

1 whole head of garlic
2¼ pounds Desiree or King Edward
  potatoes, peeled and cut into
  even-sized pieces
½ cup milk
3½ ounces butter
2 tablespoons mascarpone
salt flakes and freshly ground
  black pepper
freshly grated nutmeg

4 PINCHED PERSIAN RICE

This adapted and adopted dish formed part of my childhood and is just too delicious not to include–not least because of how wonderfully it goes with the grills on pages 118–33.

Put the rice in a sieve and rinse until the water runs clear. Let drain.

Put 3 cupfuls of water in a pan with the salt, butter, cardamom, and lemon peel. Bring to a boil. When boiling, add the rice and stir with a fork. Wrap a clean tea towel around the lid of the pan and cover the rice with it. Lower the heat and cook until all the water has evaporated, about 20–30 minutes.

While the rice is cooking, make the topping: heat some oil in a frying pan and cook the onion. When it begins to color, add the raisins and almonds. Season with salt and pepper, and take care not to burn the raisins.

When the rice is nice and fluffy, and all the water has been absorbed (and the bottom begins to crisp up), spread it out on a large warmed serving dish, and top with onion and raisin mixture. Sprinkle with the chopped mint.

TASTY TRANSFORMATION
Make the topping using pistachios instead of almonds and adding chopped apricots and a sprinkling of crushed rose petals.

2 cups basmati rice
½ teaspoon rock salt
1 ounce butter
3 cardamom pods
1 piece of lemon peel

FOR THE TOPPING
olive oil
1 large onion, thinly sliced
generous handful of raisins or barberries
generous handful of kibbled or roughly
  chopped blanched almonds
salt flakes and freshly ground
  black pepper
handful of chopped fresh mint

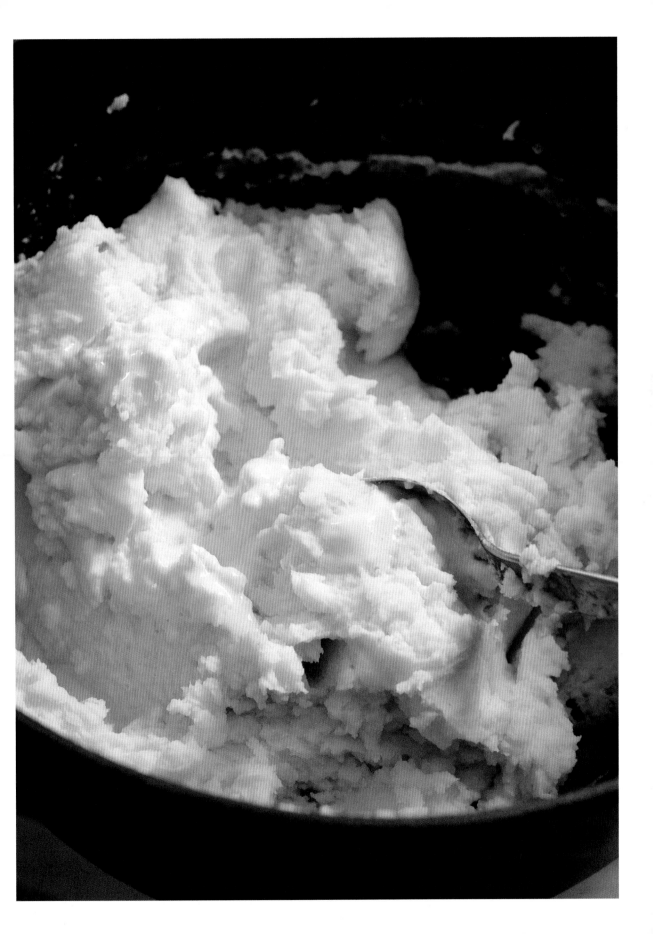

5 SALAD DAYS & SALAD SECRETS

Raw is the key to healthy life, therefore I suggest fresh organic raw vegetable combinations as a key part of an Easy Tasty life.

'A spendthrift for the oil, a miser for the vinegar, a sage for the salt, and a madman to mix.' *Dr. Strauss's Cookery Book, Dishes and Drinks or Philosophy in the Kitchen*, published in 1887.

Add your own madness to the method. I have led the way with a couple of crazy combinations below to get you started.

I never make dressing on the side but dress over the bowl. To the right are my preferred ingredients.

NOTE I often sprinkle salads with Furikake stardust (page 39) or mixed seeds for a nutritious extra nutty flavor.

extra virgin olive oil
one of the following: wine vinegar,
   balsamic vinegar, lemon juice,
   flavored vinegars, etc.
salt flakes and freshly ground
   black pepper
1 healthy pinch of madness

6 SANTINI SALAD

Misticanza is a mix of salad leaves and herbs such as borage and mint.

Arrange the leaves over 4 plates, then arrange the bocconcini and melon chunks over them. Scatter with the strawberry quarters and almonds, then dress with the oil and vinegar, and season well.

14 ounces misticanza (mixed leaf salad)
12 bocconcini di mozzarella di buffala,
   torn into chunks
1 cantaloupe melon, peeled, deseeded,
   and diced
1 punnet of strawberries, quartered
handful of toasted flaked almonds
6 tablespoons olive oil
2 tablespoons sherry vinegar
salt flakes and freshly ground
   black pepper

7 SANTINI CHOPPED SALAD

Dice all the ingredients to the size of a thumbnail.
Mix well and dress as above.

2 grilled chicken breasts
5 ounces pancetta
2 avocados, peeled and stoned
2 beef tomatoes
2 Granny Smith apples
1 large can of sweetcorn kernels
   (preferably salad-crisp version),
   drained
2 romaine lettuces

8 LUCKY LENTILS

Lentils are considered to be lucky in Italy and always eaten on New Year's Eve as an auspicious way to bring luck and money. I eat them all the year round, for good measure!

Place the lentils in a sieve and rinse well (checking for stones as you do so).

Heat the oil in a shallow pan and sauté the onion and garlic until soft and glassy. Add the lentils and herbs, and sauté with the onion. Add a ladleful of stock, cover, and leave to absorb over a low heat. As the liquid is absorbed, keep adding more stock until the lentils are cooked but still retain a bite.

Remove from the heat, season, and add a further drizzle of olive oil and a squeeze of lemon juice. Serve tepid or cold.

1 pound Puy lentils
olive oil
1 onion, finely chopped
1 garlic clove, peeled and cut in half
3 kaffir lime leaves or 3 sprigs of tarragon
about 4–5 cups vegetable stock
*   (made with 2 vegetable stock cubes)*
salt flakes and freshly ground black
*   pepper*
juice of 1 lemon

9 ROLL, WRAP, & SPLASH POTATOES

Preheat the oven to 245°F. Place the potatoes in salted boiling water and reduce the heat to a simmer, cover, and par-cook for 5–8 minutes or until the outer edge only is fluffy. Drain in a colander and jiggle until the outside edges are all fluffed up. Toss in the Parmesan and roll each potato in prosciutto. Place in a roasting pan with your chosen herb, a good dousing of olive oil, some salt and lots of black pepper, and roast until crisp and golden. If you think life is too short to wrap a potato, the prosciutto can just be roughly chopped and strewn over the cheesy potatoes with the herbs.

2 pounds roasting potatoes, peeled
*   and cut into 1-inch pieces*
3 ounces Parmesan cheese
5 ounces prosciutto di Parma slices
½ ounce fresh sage or rosemary
olive oil
salt flakes and freshly ground black pepper

10 U-MAMMA! PEAS & PANCETTA

Italian mushy peas with bacon!

Heat a glug of oil in a large frying pan and sauté the pancetta in it. When cooked through, add the onion slices. Sauté until the onion begins to color and the pancetta begins to crisp up. Add the peas to the pan with the mint, season with salt and pepper and leave to cook on a very low heat for a couple of minutes with the lid on.

olive oil
3 ounces pancetta, diced
1 onion, thinly sliced
two 7-ounce cans of petit pois
*   (try to get the ones in water, salt*
*   and sugar), drained and rinsed*
sprig of fresh mint, torn
salt flakes and freshly ground black
*   pepper*

12 QUICK
& EASY
DESSERTS

All recipes in this section serve 4.

1 THE FINGER

Give your guests the finger with this new approach to a traditional tiramisu.
I always find myself scooping the cream from around the biscuits, so I just left the one.

To prepare the magic fingers: melt the chocolate in a bain-marie and dip the end of each biscuit in the chocolate; decorate with gold leaf if using it. Set aside to dry in a cool place. Prepare the espresso coffee, add a splash of whisky (or whiskey), if using it, and chill.

Whisk the egg yolks with sugar until pale and thick. Add the vanilla essence and fold in the mascarpone and coffee grains until smooth. Whisk the egg whites until stiff and carefully fold into the mascarpone mixture, taking care not to lose much of the air. If not serving immediately, cover and refrigerate; stir before using.

To assemble, pour 2 tablespoons of the chilled coffee into each glass, add a large dollop of the mascarpone cream mixture, add the finger, and dust with cocoa powder and coffee beans.

½ cup strong espresso coffee, chilled
* and sweetened to taste*
splash of whisky or whiskey (optional)
3 eggs, separated
3 tablespoons superfine sugar
¼ teaspoon vanilla extract
½ pound mascarpone
2 teaspoons ground coffee beans
cocoa powder for dusting

FOR THE MAGIC FINGERS
2 ounces melted dark chocolate
* (70% cacao)*
4 Savoiardi sponge fingers
edible gold leaf (page 40, optional)

2 LEMON & LAVENDER POSSET

Place the cream and sugar in a pan and bring to a boil; simmer for 3 minutes. Remove from heat and stir in lemon zest and juice. Leave to cool for a few minutes, before pouring into serving glasses. Decorate each glass with a sprinkle of lavender.

Serve with Lavender and rosemary wands.

2 cups heavy cream
4 ounces superfine sugar
juice and finely grated zest of 2 lemons
2 teaspoons dried lavender flowers
4 Lavender and rosemary wands
* (page 181), to serve*

3 CHILI CHOCOLATE ORANGE MOUSSE

Melt the chocolate in a bain-marie and set aside. Whisk the whole eggs with the sugar until thick and voluminous. When the mixture can hold a figure-of-eight, carefully fold in the melted chocolate, a pinch of chili powder if using, and the orange zest and juice. This produces a wonderful rich velvety mouse.

Serve with a dollop of whipped cream and Chocolate chili grissini wands.

VARIATION Replace the chili and orange with crushed rose petals and a pinch of crushed red peppercorns, using lime instead of orange.

7 ounces dark chocolate 70% cocoa
* or chili chocolate 70%*
3 large eggs
2 ounces unrefined superfine sugar
pinch of chili powder (optional
* if using chili chocolate)*
grated zest of 1 orange and 4 tablespoons of
* juice*

TO SERVE (OPTIONAL)
whipped cream
4 Chocolate chili grissini wands (page 181)

4 SOPHIA LOREN'S RICOTTA CONDITA

This simple dressed ricotta recipe is adapted from one by the original *Dea Domestica* (Domestic Goddess), Sophia Loren in her book, *In Cucina con Amore*, where she talks of Peter Sellers being won over by this creamy dessert. Birdie Yum Yum!

Mix the ricotta with the sugar and cocoa (the quantities here for sugar and cocoa are just indications, and you must make it to your own taste). Splash with brandy if you like.

VARIATIONS You can also dress ricotta with:
Chocolate chips with chopped candied fruit and zest
Sugar, ground coffee, and whisk(e)y
A little runny honey, cinnamon, and a splash of herbal or fruit liqueur
(I often serve this with a chopped fruit salad.)

1 pound ricotta
4 tablespoons caster sugar
4 tablespoons unsweetened cocoa powder
splash of brandy

5 PARMESAN ICE CREAM WITH BALSAMIC STRAWBERRIES & BLACK PEPPER

This recipe is an edible gift most generously given by Caroline & Robin Weir from their book, *Ice Creams, Sorbet & Gelati*. With origins in the 17th century, this recipe is an ingenious way of getting 'savory deliciousness' to cross the line into sweet indulgence. It's a very hard line to cross, but once crossed, there is no going back.

Bring the cream to a boil with the sugar, stirring constantly. Then remove from the heat and add the grated Parmesan cheese, stirring until it melts. Allow to cool, then scrape into a freezer box, cover, and freeze overnight.

Serve with chopped strawberries, a grinding of black pepper, a drizzle of sticky balsamic vinegar and 100% Cacao & parmesan wands.

NOTE Use only Parmigiano-Reggiano, as I am afraid cheaper versions are too chalky for this delicate cream.

2 cups whipping cream
4 ounces golden organic granulated sugar
4 ounces finely grated Parmesan cheese
1¼ pounds ripe strawberries, chopped
freshly ground black pepper
1 tablespoon good aged balsamic vinegar
four 100% Cacao & parmesan wands
  (optional, page 181)

The world doesn't terrify me. Just the people.

Donny Miller

6 FROZEN GRAPES

It does not get more simple or stylish.

Wash the grapes well, taking care not to dislodge any from the bunch. Place on a flat surface and put in the freezer to freeze.

Remove the grapes from the freezer just before serving in order to maintain the dewy bloom. Serve with a plate of good chocolates, some strong espresso coffee, and iced liqueurs if you like.

1 good-looking bunch of grapes (white or red)
an assortment of good chocolates, to serve
some strong espresso coffee, to serve
chilled grappa or any other after-dinner liqueur(s) (optional)

7 BLUE LAVENDER

Something old, something new, something borrowed, something blue…

Place the blueberries in a bowl and cover with gin. Add a couple of squeezes of lime juice and a couple of pieces of peel, a pinch of lavender, and a sprinkling of sugar to taste. Mix well, cover, and refrigerate. I like to sprinkle the berries with edible silver and serve with White chocolate & lavender wands.

4 punnets of firm blueberries
1¼ cups gin
juice and a couple of pieces of peel from 1 lime
pinch of dried lavender flowers
caster sugar
edible silver (optional, page 40)
4 White chocolate & lavender wands (optional, page 181)

TASTY TRANSFORMATION
Strawberries with red wine, mint, and lemon is as refreshing as it is boozy. Remove the stalks from 4 punnets of ripe strawberries, quarter lengthwise, place in a bowl and pour in a bottle of red wine. Add sugar and lemon juice to taste, together with a couple of pieces of the lemon peel and a handful of torn mint leaves. Mix well, cover, and refrigerate.

8 GREAT BALLS OF FIRE!

You need a funnel for this. No, you don't sit on the watermelon and put the funnel in your mouth… but make a hole in the top of the watermelon, give it a drink of vodka, wait for it to sink in and put it back in the refrigerator. Keep topping it up over a few days and bingo! Bite into the laced red flesh and…what a thrill!

1 large ripe watermelon
1 bottle of vodka

NOTE Not to be cut around children.

9 GRISSINI WANDS & MAGIC FINGERS

Melt the chocolate over a bain-marie, dip the grissini in it to just under half their length and then sprinkle with your choice of decoration. Leave to dry in a cool place, standing upright in a row of glasses.

SOME MAGICAL IDEAS
White chocolate with lavender and edible silver
White chocolate with violet and edible silver
70% dark chocolate with chili flakes and edible gold or Chocolate & chili stardust (page 39)
70% dark chocolate with crushed rose petals, pink peppercorns, and edible gold or Rose stardust (page 39)
Parmesan and bitter chocolate with lavender

NOTE For savory wands, use 100% cacao and dip in chili, tasty seeds, herbs, and even Parmesan, and plenty of gold and silver (page 40).

MAGIC FINGERS
Manicure sponge fingers in exactly the same way.

1 pack of thin grissini
about 3 ounces chocolate (dark, milk, white... your choice)

FOR THE SPRINKLES
crushed chili, dried lavender flowers, crushed rose, violet, edible gold or silver (page 40), grated Parmesan cheese ...

10 BARONE VERDE—THE GREEN BARON

The inspiration for this comes from Yauatcha, a dim sum restaurant in London's Soho that is a temple of style and deliciousness, and one of my favourite places to chow down in the world. I worked this ridiculously quick recipe out when another, far more complicated, sorbet recipe went wrong and I needed a quick fix. I have not looked back since. This is true alchemy and guests' reactions always outweigh the sum of the ingredients that go into this.

Sneak away from the table and remove the sorbet from the freezer about 10 minutes before serving. When ready to serve, tip the sorbet into a tall container, add the basil and alcohol splash, and blitz with a hand blender for a second or two.

Spoon into glasses and serve with a wafer, biscuit or wand on the side. Take care not to blitz too much, as this will make it runny rather than the whippy consistency in the picture.

NOTE I have also tried this with Tequila and mint and a fresh green chili pepper. The options are endless: raspberry and framboise, coconut or mango, and Malibu with cilantro. I have not moved on to ice creams yet, but will let you know when I do.

2 cups good-quality lemon sorbet
2 ounces fresh basil leaves
generous splash of Martini Bianco or vodka

11 PIMP YOUR PLATE

This is a trick I learned from my great friend Lorna Wing, the woman who put the 'ate' into UK outside catering. All you need are some good props and away you go. I spend my life in flea markets and charity shops, pimping my collection.

SWEET HOUSE MIX

Choose a theme: chocolate, fruit, coffee, etc.
Fill 4 shot glasses with an after-dinner liqueur, anything from Vin Santo to the Angel water on page 184.
Fill 4 tea glasses (Moroccan ones are both economical and beautiful) with a good-quality ice cream, sorbet, or granita.
Place one of each glass on 4 pretty plates, together with a special chocolate, a piece of patisserie or cantucci, and finish off with a pretty teaspoon or long-handled sundae spoon, and a grissini wand.
The result is a magical sensory feast. Ideas are endless; use the photograph opposite to inspire you and pimp away!

CHEESY HOUSE MIX

Use the same idea to make an inspiring cheese plate. Fill the shot glasses with port or a good cheese wine. Place Parmesan ice cream (page 176), chopped strawberries and a drizzle of balsamic vinegar in the tea glasses, or just some simple celery ribs. Experiment with honeys, nuts, and chutneys. Mix blue cheese and mascarpone or chunks of Parmesan drizzled with thick balsamic vinegar, frozen grapes, and 100% cacao chocolate Grissini wands (page 181).

4 pretty plates
4 small shot glasses
4 tea glasses (Moroccan ones are both economical and beautiful)
4 pretty teaspoons or long-handled sundae spoons

12 DREAMY CARAMEL CLOUDS WITH CUT FRUIT & FLOWERS

Whip the cream so that it is still soft but can hold a peak. Very lightly sweeten with a little icing sugar or rose sugar, a drop of vanilla essence, and a splash of booze, if using. Set aside. Note that flavoring the cream is actually optional and this works just as well without.

Cut the fruit into large chunks, about 1-inch pieces, and add a squeeze of lemon or lime juice and a sprinkling of sugar to stop it browning. Arrange the fruit on a large flat platter and cover in fluffy clouds of whipped cream, then refrigerate.

Put the superfine sugar in a heavy-based pan and cook over a medium heat. When the sugar begins to melt and come away from the sides, give the pan a good shake and continue to cook as more begins to melt. Give it another shake or stir with a wooden spoon, and continue to cook until it is all liquid. Take off the heat when the sugar looks like runny honey, as it will continue cooking.

NOTE Caramel is really hot and can give you a nasty burn; not to be made when you are dolly daydreaming.

Pour the caramel in zig-zags across the top of your cream clouds. Sprinkle with pounded rose petals, chopped pistachios, fresh mint leaves, and cinnamon. For some Alvin Stardust, I like to give my clouds a silver lining and sprinkle with silver flakes.

4 cups whipping cream
icing sugar or rose sugar
drop of vanilla essence
splash of brandy or rum (optional)
assorted fresh fruit, such as banana, pear, pineapple, apple, berries, passion fruit, star fruit, orange, peeled as necessary
juice of 1 lemon or lime
6 ounces white superfine sugar
1 tablespoon crystallized rose petals or violets
handful of chopped pistachio nuts
1 sprig of fresh mint leaves
pinch of ground cinnamon
silver flakes (optional, page 40)

SPIRIT & ETHER: THE FIFTH ELEMENT

Sometimes we use the intoxicating tools of the fifth element to dare to be who we truly are. For real intoxication, dare to be who you are sober.

Throw your dreams into space like a kite, and you do not know what it will bring back, a new life, a new friend, a new love, a new country. Anaïs Nin

I had a little nut tree, nothing would it bear
But a silver nutmeg and a golden pear;
The King of Spain's daughter came to visit me,
And all was because of my little nut tree.
I skipped over water, I danced over sea,
And all the birds in the air couldn't catch me.
'Little Nut Tree', Unknown.

AQUA DEGLI ANGELI (ANGEL WATER—THE ELIXIR OF LIFE)

Take a bottle of any high-alcohol clear spirit, such as vodka, grappa, eau-de-vie, etc. Drop in a lucky red chili pepper and a generous pinch of edible gold flakes (page 40). This makes a truly magical gift fit for kings and queens.

RHUBARBCELLO

This recipe was given to me by Kitchen Revolutionary, Rosie Sykes.

2 pounds rhubarb, chopped
8-14 ounces sugar
sticky inners of 1 split
 vanilla pod
4 cups vodka

Put all the ingredients in a jar and leave in a cool dark place for 6 weeks.

Strain through a fine mesh (I use 10 dernier tights) and you will have a prettily colored but lethal rhubarb vodka or 'Rhubarbcello' as we nicknamed it.

Serve with biscotti at the end of a meal and it won't be long before the whole table is talking rhubarb!

TASTY TRANSFORMATION

Replace rhubarb with chopped quince, a stick of cinnamon, and a nutmeg. Once strained, add some flecks of edible gold and silver (see page 40).

SGROPPINO

This classic Venetian cocktail is traditionally served after dinner. Don't be fooled by its soft and slushy appearance; this puppy bites!

1¼ cups lemon sorbet
8 ice cubes
1 glass of vodka
1 cup Prosecco or any dry
 sparkling wine

TO DECORATE
grated lemon zest
edible silver flakes (page 40)

Whiz all the ingredients in a blender until thick and fluffy.

Pour into iced Champagne glasses and decorate with grated lemon zest and a sprinkle of silver.

ROSEMARY PUCINO

This botanical cocktail recipe was very kindly created specially for this book by fellow alchemists, the Soil Sisters. It was upon their potent alchemic altar, that I set eyes on some of the most beautiful organic potions I have ever seen. These high priestesses of the soil capture the genies of the aromatic world and preserve them in Rainbow Spirits: heady botanical kaleidoscopes to be sipped and savored.

Try this zesty, revitalizing, pink-hued Prosecco cocktail mixed from a base of rosemary syrup and blackberry vodka. To add enjoyment, dare to wear your finest plumage! In the spirit of the Soil Sisters, all the ingredients should preferably be organic.

At least 2 months ahead, make the blackberry vodka: put the blackberries in a large clean jar or bottle. Add the sugar and vodka. Secure with a lid and give a good shake. Shake daily for the next week, then leave in a cool place for 7 weeks. Pass the mixture through a fine sieve, then pour the strained mixture into bottles, and seal.

At least a day ahead, make the rosemary syrup: put the sugar and 2½ cups water in a pan and dissolve it over a gentle heat, then bring to a boil. Lower the heat and simmer gently for 2 minutes. Remove from the heat and add the rosemary. Let infuse for 24 hours.

Next day, bring the syrup back to a boil. Remove from the heat and strain into a jug. Using a funnel, pour the hot syrup into sterilized bottles. Seal. The syrup will keep in the refrigerator for up to 3 months.

To mix this botanical cocktail, blend one part each of the rosemary syrup and the vodka, then top up with Prosecco. To each glass, add a long sprig of rosemary, a blackberry, and a couple of ice cubes or some crushed ice.

TASTY TRANSFORMATION
Create your own botanical cocktails using your own blend of petals, herbs, and spices.

1 part Blackberry vodka
  (see below)
1 part Rosemary syrup
  (see below)
4 parts chilled Prosecco
long fresh rosemary sprigs
fresh blackberries
ice cubes or crushed ice

FOR THE BLACKBERRY VODKA
1 pound blackberries
1 tablespoon sugar
2½ cups vodka

FOR THE ROSEMARY SYRUP
1 pound sugar
2 fresh rosemary branches, each about
  6 inches long

INDEX

CREDITS

Front cover frame © MaRoDee Photography/Alamy; 10 Laura Santtini;
13 © Olive Sandwiches/www.olivesandwiches.com; 19 © www.purpose.co.uk;
21 © Linda Lieberman 'Soulmate 01'; 23 © Christopher Scholey; 26 © Conny Jude;
34 © Andrea Kett 2009; 36 © Alfred Wertheimer/photokunst; 46 © Christopher Scholey;
49 Laura Santtini; 75 © Christopher Scholey; 82 © Sean Gleason (customized chef's jacket
by Robin's Jean); 134 © www.purpose.co.uk; 145 © Rupert Sanderson;
176 © Donny Miller; 192 Laura Santtini

ACKNOWLEDGMENTS
A special thank you to all the staff and customers at Santini
who have supported my endeavors with such enthusiasm.
Enormous thanks also to all the following:

My father, Gino Santin, a remarkable restaurateur and natural master of umami;
my mother Maggie Santin; David and Sandy Scholey; Fiorenza; Goli; Janie; Lyn;
Gillian Riley, whose work has been an inspiration and for writing such a special
foreword, every word a feast; Richard Thompson at Merlin Elite for being brilliant;
Alison Cathie for opening her doors to golden angels and golden pasta; Jane O'Shea
with great respect and affection for marshaling this book from within; Lewis Esson,
my editor with the Midas touch, for his kindness, unfaltering support, guidance,
and scrupulous understanding of food. Simon Wheeler, the gentleman photographer,
whose unspoilt work and impeccable eye speaks for itself; Helen Lewis and
Jim Smith for making my paper dreams into a published reality way more than
the sum of its parts; Giles Redmayne; Rob Howsam and Charlotte Cline at Purpose,
for capturing my first dreams on paper; Sean Gleason for a wonderful cover shot;
Clare Lattin, Ian West, Melanie Gray, and all at Quadrille who worked on this book;
Isabel Entwhistle for being a dream assistant and friend; Luca Lamari and Giuseppe
Rosselli for helping me always; Lorna Wing, Lesley Sendall, and Molly Wheeler
for that hot and strange Saturday!; the wonderful Anna Del Conte, with great
admiration and gratitude; Giorgio Locatelli for his brilliant work and accepting to
read this book on his holiday; Matthew Fort, for his genuine passion and depth of
knowledge of Italian food; Lidia Bastianich and her awe-inspiring work in Italian
food in the USA, for receiving this project with interest and warmth; Robin and
Jean-Michel at Robin's Jean, for giving me my golden wings; Sarah Canet at Spoon
PR for UK publicity and for Kim Yorio at YC Media for US publicity; Andrea Kett,
Conny Jude, Linda Lieberman, Donny Miller, and Christopher Scholey for their art;
Priscilla Santini for her lips; Maureen Mills, to whom I owe so much; Ewan Venters
at Selfridges for his incredible support, and visionary approach to food retail; William
Sitwell and WFI for championing me; Clare Blampied of Sacla UK, for her support
and all the generous opportunities; Robert Bean for thought for food; Janice Gabriel
and the team at Market Kitchen; Mark Bushnell, Madeleine Clarke, Rokelle Lerner,
and Rusty for passing me the tools; The Angels, Estelle Bingham, Angela Donovan,
Carla Lelli, Barbara Olive, Sylvie Targhetta, and Yvonne Williams; Sheuneen,
Jose, and Bella at Neville for making me feel good; Charlotte Ribeyro for make-up;
Cheryl Konteh for styling; Louise Chatwyn; Vincenzo Zaccarini at Vincenzo Ltd
for bringing the tastes of Italy to London; Ewan at the Lacquer Chest for magical
props, tea-lc, and cake; Sandra Manenti; Patrick O'Hara; Dawn Gregory; Tanya
McMullen; Sasha Notley; Nancy Wainscoat; Pooja Sharma; Mike Small; Belinda
Herden; Pimula; Charlotte, Lia, Cora, and Luca; Josie; Louis. To anyone I may
have forgotten, please forgive me and know that this is you.

In loving memory of Catherine.

EPILOGUE

I have learned that life is an ever-transforming recipe: the people are the ingredients, the circumstances the cooking methods and when we can't stand the heat we yearn to get out of the kitchen. Sofia Loren refers to her husband as a little meat roll '*Mio marito e un "involtino"*' in the epilogue of her book and goes on to divulge that every time she meets someone new she associates them with a dish. When I began to write this book I was burnt toast; today as I contemplate my summer vacation, I feel like a wobbly blancmange. But yesterday I felt truly delicious. Who knows what I will be tomorrow...

Remember your life is your larder in this world: taste everything, spit out the unpalatable, savor the sweet, and search for the umami. *Buon appetito*!

WWW.LAURASANTTINI.COM

To source some of the more specialist ingredients online:
www.steenbergs.co.uk (for fine organic and Fairtrade foods)
www.thespiceshop.co.uk
www.selfridges.com (for edible noble metals)